THE CHAKRA COMPENDIUM

A BEGINNER'S GUIDE TO ACTIVATING, BALANCING AND HEALING YOUR CHAKRA SYSTEM.

ALEXANDRA RUDOWSKI

© Copyright 2019 - All rights reserved.

It is not legal to reproduce, duplicate, or transmit any part of this document in either electronic means or in printed format. Recording of this publication is strictly prohibited and any storage of this document is not allowed unless with written permission from the publisher except for the use of brief quotations in a book review.

INTRODUCTION

The secret to achieving perfect health, emotional wellbeing and attaining your purpose in life lies in having healthy and well-aligned chakras. For millennia, Buddhist monks and the ancient Chinese used the knowledge of chakras to live happy, meaningful lives of fulfillment and spiritual alignment. They attained mastery of their bodies and emotions and had a clear idea of their purpose in life. Fortunately, this ancient knowledge has also made it to the West over the course of the last decade, so you can also use these practices to gain control over your life and develop a deeper connection to your body, mind, and soul.

While the ancient knowledge about the chakras can be life-changing, there is one major problem. Within our society, there is a lack of quality-cited, information on the subject that all cater to a variety of different contexts. The literature currently available on chakras focuses too much on "new-age" arguments and views while ignoring the actual content that can help you align your body, mind, and soul and live a happy and enlightened life.

INTRODUCTION

If you feel that the connection to these portions of yourself is out of alignment and don't know how to realign yourself, this book has the solution for you. **The chakra system** is a tool that people have used for thousands of years to achieve exactly what you have been searching for, and in this book, you will learn detailed and concise information about the history of the chakra system, what they are, how history has interpreted them, and how to use them in a modern world.

The book will also provide you with valuable solutions in the form of techniques, meditations, and information that will empower you to become successfully in tune with your mind, body, and spirit using the chakra system. By the time you finish this book, you will have a substantial understanding of your chakra system and will be capable of developing a deeper connection with your inner self.

The author of this book, **Alexandra Rudowski**, has already gained a reputation for herself as an expert Eastern tradition. Rudowski was raised as an atheist. She has a bachelor's degree in biology and has believed logic and reason above all else from a very young age. Rudowski's journey with the chakra system started when she began meditating at fifteen. Owing to her upbringing, she was always skeptical of the usefulness and existence of the chakra system; however, through the practices and techniques that she studied and developed over the previous two decades, she has been able to fully and successfully integrate the chakra system into her life.

Rudowski is deeply passionate about helping others live their best lives, and her ultimate mission is to provide people with the tools they need to deepen their spiritual connection with themselves, achieve a sense of clarity and purpose in their lives, and live happy, meaningful lives of fulfillment and spiritual alignment.

So far, Rudowski has helped hundreds of people achieve the same success she has achieved through the classes she has taught over the past seven years. She has influenced many people close to her to lead more fulfilling and effective lives by taking advantage of the chakra system.

If you are still skeptical about the effectiveness of the chakra system, it may also surprise you to learn that some of the most successful people in the world use some form of meditation—a prominent practice in the chakra system. Some successful people who practice meditation include Jack Dorsey, Oprah Winfrey, Russell Simmons, Jim Carrey, Ellen DeGeneres, Cameron Diaz, Katy Perry, Bill Gates, Curtis Jackson, Ray Dalio, Kendrick Lamar, Kobe Bryant, Michael Jordan, Clint Eastwood, Hugh Jackman, Paul McCartney, Will Smith, Russell Brand, Joe Rogan, Aubrey Marcus, among many others. The chakra system provides you with a useful visualization tool as a supplement to meditation, and by taking advantage of what you learn in this book, you will have the potential to unlock the same levels of productivity and abundance as the people mentioned above.

Some benefits you will gain from this book include having a happier, more meaningful, and spiritually aligned life while achieving a sense of purpose and clarity in your life. The tools in this book will give you the strength and fortitude you need to tackle the hard challenges that life throws at you, even those you were unwilling to face before. You will become better at performing under stress and navigating the most difficult situations. Ultimately, you will also become more aware of your mind and body, which will make it easier for you to carry out smarter and more effective decisions, leading to a healthier mind and body.

There have also been various studies into the subject. A study done by Fernros et al. (2009) found that well-educated men and women could increase their life satisfaction and quality of life by using various chakra healing techniques (i.e. meditation and yoga). Younger people were also able to decrease their use of psychoactive drugs (i.e. sleeping pills, SSRIs) during and after the study. Maxwell (2009) researched yoga chakra expression, and theorized that we can enhance our yoga practices by incorporating chakra healing practices into them.

In 1983, Gallegos studied visualization techniques connected to chakras, animals, and psychotherapy of patients. He would ask clients to focus on a particular portion of the body (that which connects to a specific chakra) during their psychotherapy sessions. He would then ask the patient to turn their thoughts into an animal, and describe what the animal was doing. When comparing the animals chosen by the patients, he found that many of the animals correlated to the chakras also had similar characteristics, evidence of the existence of chakras and how we can all feel their energies on similar wavelengths.

Achieving the benefits of the chakra system and unlocking the life you desire will be difficult and may take you years. I do not mean this to discourage you, but instead, it should motivate you to learn as much as you can so you can unlock your highest potential. With expert guidance, you can reach this state.

Every chapter in this book will provide you with actionable and tangible steps that will empower you to activate, heal, and balance all chakras in your body. It will serve as an

INTRODUCTION

encouraging tool to audit your life with courage and ask yourself the tough questions associated with specific chakras. It will help you gain deeper and higher levels of awareness and capabilities, as long as you are honest with yourself and take the necessary action. You will learn about many techniques that can stimulate a greater awareness of your chakras, such as implementing specific fragrances, activities, and mantras. This book will also provide you with guided meditations that will allow you to visualize and feel your chakras at a much deeper level than you have ever been able to achieve.

Ready to embark on a journey that will change your life? Let's dive in!

CHAPTER ONE: HISTORY OF THE CHAKRA SYSTEM

Over the last century, there has been a growing interest in various Eastern traditions. Among these Eastern traditions is **the chakra system**—one of the most popular in the West and is the concept of subtle energy centers. But what exactly is a chakra, and where did this system originate?

ALEXANDRA RUDOWSKI

Chakras of the subtle body, folio 2 from the Nath Charit. Attributed to Bulaki, 1823. Mehrangarh Museum

The literal meaning of the word **chakra** is a "spinning wheel" or "disk." Originally, the term chakra was used regarding the chariot wheels of the *cakravartin*, the ancient rulers who ruled over India. Practitioners also used the word chakra metaphorically to refer to the sun, which glides across the sky like the chariots of the *cakravartin*. This metaphor references the *kalacakra*, which is the eternal wheel of time.

In **tantric traditions**, however, from which the chakra system originated, chakra refers specifically to spinning wheels or disks of energy found within the human body, particularly along the spine.

To understand the concept of chakra, it is good to understand the role of energy in the universe. Everything in this world and in the entire universe contains energy—the sun, the stars, the moon, the ocean tides, the television playing in your living room, the device you are reading this book on, and even yourself. Energy is a basic life force and constantly flows through and around your body.

According to Indian yogic traditions and traditional Chinese medicine, this energy travels across your body through invisible lines and pathways. These invisible pathways are *nadis*, and there are tens of thousands of them running through the human body. We would locate chakras at the points where there is a high convergence of *nadis* within the body. If you think of *nadis* as streets, chakras would be the intersections where several of these streets come together. Like mini energy-routers within the body, the chakras receive and transmit energy between our bodies, other people, and the surrounding environment, made up of various energy fields.

We find these chakras at points along the human spine where the nervous system branches out into sub-branches serving different parts of the body. Some traditions also describe chakras as various degrees of consciousness.

THE CHAKRA COMPENDIUM

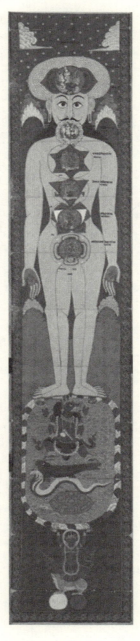

The subtle body and the cosmic man , Nepal, 1600s National Museum, New Delhi. Ajit Mookerjee Collection

It is good to note that chakras are not physical structures. If you undergo surgery or a doctor observes you using various body imaging techniques, the doctor will not find any structure in your body that they can refer to as a *chakra*. Instead, chakras are *conceptual structures* that represent how people interact with spiritual and emotional energy. However, that they are conceptual structures does not make them any less real. For instance, we know that thoughts are real, but if a neurosurgeon opens up your brain, they will not identify any physical characteristics in your brain that they can attribute to as *thought*. In the same way, though chakras may not be a physical phenomenon, they are as real as the thoughts running through your mind this very minute. A good illustration of chakras is the feeling you pick up in your gut whenever you feel worried or anxious.

The role of chakras is to hold and maintain the balance of life-energy (also referred to as *Prana*, *chi*, or *Shakti*) around their respective spheres. When one's chakras are *well-balanced*, they will experience physical, mental, emotional, and spiritual wellbeing. When the chakras are *out-of-balance*, it manifests itself through various physical and psychological symptoms.

Origin of the Chakra System

So, where did the chakra system come from, and for how

long has it existed? The concept of chakras originated in ancient India. The earliest mention of the term was found in the Vedas, which are the oldest texts containing Indian traditions written between 1500 and 500 BC. The Vedas recorded various Indian and Hindu rituals that ancient practitioners had previously passed orally from one generation to another. However, in the Vedas, the term *chakra* does not precisely refer to the subtle energy centers within the body. Instead, the term was regarding the *cakravartin* who ruled over India, "turning the wheels of their empire" in all directions as a representation of the *cakravartin's* power and influence.

The concept of chakras as energy centers was also mentioned as *"cakra"* in the various Upanishads of Hinduism, including the Cudamini Upanishad, the Shri Jabala Darshana Upanishad, the Shandilya Upanishad, and the Yoga-Shikha Upanishad. However, according to Gavin Flood, Oxford University professor of Hindu Studies and Comparative Religion, the concept of *cakra* as mentioned in the Upanishads is not precisely the same as we have in the modern chakra system.

Various Buddhist traditions since the medieval era have also used the concept of subtle energy centers. In Buddhist esoteric traditions, the number of chakras in the body varied between three and six, while many schools of Tibetan Buddhism argued that there are between four and ten main chakras. However, the most common traditions suggest four chakras, named based on their location. These are the navel (*manipura*), heart (*anahata*), throat (*vishuddha*), and crown (*ushnisha Kamala*).

According to some experts, Buddha did not directly mention chakras in his teachings, though exercises associated with chakra are clear in many of his mindfulness practices. For instance, in the mindfulness of breathing exercises (*anapanasati*), students are asked to focus their attention on the diaphragm. In the "mindfulness rooted in the body" exercise (*kayagata-sati*) students would focus more of their attention on the feelings around sections of the body such as the lower abdomen, the solar plexus, chest, and throat. All these are locations contain chakra.

Like we saw earlier, the concept of chakras has been a part of the Hindu tantra for ages. Just like in Buddhism, there are several theories about the arrangement or number of chakras. Some Hindu texts suggest thousands of chakras, while others mention only five, seven, or eight. However, the most popular theory in Hinduism believes in *seven* chakras. Considering that most of the chakra concepts taught in the West today came from Hinduism, it is not surprising that the seven chakra system has become the most prevalent in that area of the world.

There are also similarities between the chakra concept and concepts found in other energy management systems and exercises such as Qi-Gong, Silat, and Tai Chi. For instance, just like the chakra system, **Qi-Gong** believes that there is an esoteric energy system flowing through the body. Here, we would refer to the energy flowing through the body as *qi*. This *qi* can be compared to *Prana* in Hinduism, and it flows through meridians, similar to the *nadis*. However, besides qi, Qi-Gong also adds two other energies: **spirit energy** (*shen*) and **primordial essence** (*jing*). Qi-Gong posits that the three different energies pass through various *dantian*, which are similar to chakras. Just like chakras, we can locate the *dantian* at specific points within the body.

Concepts similar to the chakra system also exist in the traditional martial art of **Silat**, practiced within the Malay Archipelago. The similarities can be attributed to how Hindu and Buddhist concepts heavily influenced Silat. Martial artists practicing Silat try to make their movements and attacks more effective and powerful by making sure their movements are in harmony with the various chakras within their bodies.

Sir John Woodroffe (at the time under the pseudonym Arthur Avalon) wrote a book called *The Serpent Power* published in 1919, which described the concept of chakras for the first time in the West. It was a translation of various older Hindu texts and contained explanations of numerous Indian and Hindu concepts beyond chakras, including kundalini and tantric traditions.

The Seven Chakra Theory

While the concept of chakras has influences from various religions and traditions, each with its own theory about the arrangement and number of chakras, **the seven chakra theory** has become prominent in modern times. According to this theory, there are **six major chakra points** aligned along the spine, along with a **seventh energy center** at the crown not considered as a *real* chakra, though practitioners would count one nonetheless. According to Gavin Flood, the seven chakra theory first appeared in an 11th century **Kaula** work known as the **Kubjikāmata-tantra**. Sir John Woodroffe translated this seven chakra theory from the Kubjikāmata-tantra in his book *The Serpent Power*, which contributed to it becoming the dominant theory in the new-age interpretation of the chakra concept.

The seven chakra in the body. Nepalese painting, 18th century.

In the original appearance of the seven chakra theory, practitioners regarded the seven chakras as aids to meditation, helping the individual progress on a journey of spiritual ascension from the base chakra to the highest chakra. According to this ancient interpretation, dormant energy known as *kundalini* exists in the area around the bottommost chakra.

In the modern interpretation of the seven chakra theory, the chakras have specific functions within the body and control specific elements of our spiritual, emotional, mental, and physical wellbeing. The new-age interpretation also added a color system that was not in existence in ancient Indian, Hindu, and Buddhist traditions. The following are **the seven major chakras**, under the common new-age interpretation.

Root Chakra

Also referred to as **Muladhara**, this is the lowest (albeit the most powerful) chakra. We locate the root chakra **near the perineum**, at the base of the spine. It is represented by the color **red** and corresponds to the element **Earth**. Being the lowest chakra, the root chakra acts as a foundation or an anchor and helps us feel grounded within our lives and our environment and acts as a connection between us and Mother Earth.

We would associate the root chakra themes and emotions surrounding our survival, such as stability, food, physical security, financial security, and family. When the root chakra is *balanced*, we feel confident that we can handle whatever life throws at us. When the root chakra is *unbalanced*, we feel fearful, anxious, ungrounded, and intimidated, and we lose confidence in ourselves and our ability to handle the challenges of life.

Since the root chakra influences our basic survival instincts, it is responsible for our **fight-or-flight response**, which triggers whenever we feel threatened. The root chakra also symbolizes our sexuality and physical strength, and it influences our creativity, passion, and vitality.

In the body, the root chakra controls the functions around the large intestines, bones, feet, legs, the adrenal glands, including the gonads. The root chakra connects to our sense of **smell**.

Sacral Chakra

The second chakra, or the **Svadhisthana**, is in the area **around your lower abdomen**, about two inches below your navel. The sacral chakra symbolizes the **water** element within our bodies and is represented by the color **orange**.

We would associate the sacral chakra with themes such as emotions, our pleasures and desires, sexuality and reproduction, and a sense of abundance. It controls how we perceive and relate to emotions, both ours and those of other people. When the sacral chakra is *balanced*, we feel joyful, happy, passionate, creative, and compassionate towards others. When the sacral chakra is *unbalanced*, we become overly emotional, joyless, depressed, restless, overly indulgent and addicted to pleasures. An unbalanced sacral chakra can also reduce our desire for sex.

In our bodies, the sacral chakra has an influence on the function of the bladder, kidneys, lymphatic system, circulatory system, reproductive organs, pelvis, and large intestines. It connects to our sense of **taste**.

Solar Plexus Chakra

Known as the **Manipura** in Sanskrit, the solar plexus chakra is in **the upper abdomen**, about two inches above your navel. The solar plexus chakra symbolizes the element of **fire** and is represented by the color **yellow**.

The solar plexus chakra is another powerful chakra, with a great influence on our sell-will, transformation, and personal power. It also symbolizes our confidence in our abilities and therefore impacts our level of success both in the personal and professional spheres. We associate the solar plexus chakra with self-esteem, self-confidence, and self-worth. It influences your ability to be in control of your life and the situations you find yourself in. If you have ever been in a new situation and felt butterflies in your stomach, that was the effect of the solar plexus chakra.

When this chakra is *balanced*, we feel confident, cheerful, active, and energetic, allowing us to be respectful both to ourselves and to others. When this chakra is *blocked*, we feel insecure, doubtful, passive, needy, indecisive, and experience low self-esteem. If the solar plexus chakra is *excessively open*, we become aggressive, short-tempered, controlling, dominating, and will lack compassion for others.

Within our bodies, the solar plexus chakra influences the function of the adrenal glands, pancreas, muscles, and the digestive system. This chakra connects to our sense of **sight**.

Heart Chakra

The heart chakra, referred to as the **Anahata** in Sanskrit, is at **the center of the chest**. The heart chakra symbolizes the element of **air** and is represented by the color **green**.

As the name and symbolism apply, the heart chakra impacts our relationships with other people and our ability to give and receive love. We associate this chakra with joy, love, trust, forgiveness, and inner peace. In addition, the heart chakra acts as a link between the three bottom chakras, which relate to *materialism*, to the three top chakras, which relate to *spirituality*.

When the heart chakra is *unbalanced*, it fills us with negative emotions that ruin our relationships with others. When it is *weak*, we become lonely, shy, closed-off, isolated, distrustful, envious, jealous, and so on. When it is *excessive*, we become too reliant on other people, narcissistic, needy, and lose our personal boundaries.

Within the body, the heart chakra influences the function of the thymus gland, lymph nodes, the heart, lungs, and our hands and arms. This chakra connects to our sense of **touch**.

Throat Chakra

The throat chakra, or the **Vishuddi** in Sanskrit, is in **the area around the throat**. The throat chakra symbolizes the element **Ether** and is represented by the color **blue**.

The throat chakra represents our ability to express ourselves to others and our true inner voice. The throat chakra associates with communication, truth, self-expression, and judgment. It also influences our ability to listen to others and empathize with them.

When the throat chakra is *balanced*, we become capable of expressing ourselves truly and clearly. A balanced throat chakra also enhances our creative expression and artistic potential. When the throat chakra is *blocked*, we become quiet, shy, and afraid of speaking up and expressing our emotions. When the throat chakra is *excessive*, we become loud, arrogant, and poor listeners.

In the body, the throat chakra influences the function of the thyroid, parathyroid glands, throat and esophagus, neck vertebrae, shoulders, teeth, ears, and arms.

Third Eye Chakra

Also known as **Ajna**, the third eye chakra is in **the area between your eyebrows**. The term Ajna translates the "center of monitoring/knowledge" in Sanskrit. The third eye chakra symbolizes the element of **light** and is represented by the color **indigo**.

You can think of the third eye chakra as "the eye of the soul." It represents the ability to think, use logic, rationalize, and conduct analyses to come up with logical conclusions. It also represents our ability to connect to our intuition and to see information beyond what is obvious on the surface. The third eye chakra associates with intuitive wisdom, imagination, and decision-making.

People who have a *balanced* third eye chakra are usually

charismatic, charming, and wise. They are confident in themselves and are great at grasping the bigger picture in every situation. These people also have well-developed telepathic abilities. When the third eye chakra is *blocked*, people usually experience denial and poor memory. Contrarily, when it is *excessive*, they become paranoid, delusional, and find it difficult to concentrate.

In the body, the third eye chakra influences the function of the neurological system, the pineal gland, and the pituitary gland. It also affects visual perception and other aspects of telepathic communication.

Crown Chakra

This is the topmost chakra, also known as the **Sahasrara** in Sanskrit. The crown chakra is at **the top of the head**. It symbolizes the element of **consciousness** and is represented by the color **ultraviolet**.

The crown chakra is a representation of the capability to become fully connected to the spiritual realm and is associated with themes such as awareness and ultimate truth.

Someone with a perfectly *balanced* crown chakra can access higher levels of consciousness and can transcend the limitations of the physical body and laws of nature. However, it is good to note that it is difficult to achieve such a level of balance of the crown chakra, and only a few people ever get even close. People who have attained this high level of balance also have a heightened awareness of death and immortality, and there are claims that such people can even perform miracles.

When the crown chakra is *blocked*, we become spiritually cynical, depressed, and feel like we have no connection to higher realms of consciousness. When the crown chakra is *excessively open*, we feel like we have an addiction to spirituality, as if we are overly intelligent or are dissociated from our bodies.

In the body, the crown chakra influences the function of the brain, particularly the cerebral cortex, the pituitary gland, and the central nervous system.

These are the seven chakras that make up **the modern seven chakra system**. The aim for anyone who practices the chakra system is to achieve a balance of these seven chakras. When they are all aligned and spinning in harmony, one experiences physical, mental, and spiritual wellbeing. Unfortunately, for most of us, the seven chakras are not balanced. You might find that one or more of your chakras are blocked or excessively open, depending on your physical, mental or emotional state, affecting your wellbeing as outlined in the previous sections. By aligning all your chakras and ensuring there is a balance between them, you can improve your health, harness the natural energies of your body, and use them to go after what you want in life.

In the subsequent chapters, we will take a detailed look into each of the seven chakras, and also how to align each chakra.

Before we get into that, however, I want to make a disclaimer. While chakras are psycho-spiritual energy centers within the body, this **does not mean you need to be a believer in metaphysical energy fields to benefit from the chakra system.** You can still use the chakras as tools to aid your meditation exercises. As we saw earlier, some ancient traditions used the chakras as meditation aids, while other cultures and religions had their own interpretations. Therefore, what matters is not your belief in the existence of metaphysical energy fields and energy centers, but rather your own interpretation of these chakras.

CHAPTER TWO: THE ROOT CHAKRA

The **Muladhara** (also spelled as *Mooladhara*), is the first chakra that forms the base for all the others. Muladhara, the Sanskrit term for the root chakra, is a combination of two words: *mula*, meaning "root," and *adhara*, meaning "base" or "support." As a foundation for the other chakras, the root chakra derives its energy from the **Earth**, the element on which this chakra is based. The root chakra is responsible for making you feel safe and grounded. Just like the roots of a tree, the root chakra provides you with a connection to the earth and a channel through which you can draw life-giving and nourishing energies.

The symbol for the root chakra is an inverted triangle inside a square, which is then inside a red lotus flower with four cloves. Each of these elements that make up the symbol for the root chakra has a specific meaning. The following sections outline the meanings behind each of the symbols.

The Inverted Triangle

This symbol has multiple meanings. First, the inverted triangle is the alchemist symbol for Earth. Second, with the tip pointing down, the inverted triangle is a representation of the soul being seeded into the root chakra and being born in a physical form. Finally, the wide top and pointed bottom of the triangle represents the growth and expansion of consciousness from the root chakra. This implies that the root chakra provides a foundation from which human potential can blossom.

The Square

Just like the inverted triangle, the square also has multiple meanings. The first is that the square is a representation of the stability and rigidity the root chakra provides, allowing the other chakras to base on it. In addition, the four sides of the square represents the number four, which is an important figure in the physical dimension, as represented by the four physical elements, the four seasons, the four cardinal directions, and so on.

The Lotus Flower with Four Cloves

The four cloves on the lotus flower are a representation of the four main facets of the human psyche: mind, consciousness, intellect, and ego. We could also take the four cloves as a representation of the four goals of human life: having a meaningful life full of purpose (*artha*); a moral and virtuous life (*dharma*); a life dedicated to self-actualization and spiritual liberation (*Moksha*); and a life of emotional fulfillment and pleasure (*Kama*). Brought together, these four goals form one of the key concepts of Hinduism and are collectively the object of human pursuit (*Purusartha*).

The Color Red

The root chakra is characterized by the color **red**, as represented by the red lotus flower. According to Hinduism, red represents *Shakti*, which translates to mean "energy," "evolution," "movement," or "awakening." Just like dawns are red, this red symbolizes the awakening of human consciousness. In this regard, red demonstrates the root chakra as a depiction of human evolution from animal consciousness to self-awareness and spiritual awareness.

There is also another reason that red is used to represent the root chakra. Red is the densest of all the representative chakra colors, and among those that make up the visible spectrum, it has the lowest wavelength. Despite this, it is the most stimulating color to the human eye. It automatically draws our attention. Red is the first color we come into contact with after birth (in the form of blood) and is a signal of both danger and the instinct for survival, hence the reason we see it frequently on stop signs and warning signs. The tendency of the color red to command attention and stimulate our instincts is also part of why it is used to represent the root chakra, as this is the chakra that controls our instincts and primal drive.

Some characteristics associated with the root chakra include:

- Survival
- Safety and security
- Grounding
- Support (a base) from which we can grow and expand our lives
- Provision of basic needs, such as food, shelter, sleep, and sex
- Self-preservation
- Aspects of the self and physical identity

As the first energy center within the subtle body and the foundation of the other chakras, the *Prana* of the root chakra forms at conception and acts as a starting point for life. The development of the spine following conception starts at the bottom (*Mooladhara*) and moves upwards towards the crown chakra.

The root chakra is associated with survival and is therefore very instinctual. It controls the animal nature that lies inside of us and provides us with the primal energy needed for this survival.

It controls the primal energy lying inside us and ensures we satisfy all the required needs to survive, including the need for food and water, safety, emotional connection, stability, with the inclusion of fearlessness. The root chakra makes you feel safe and grounded when you meet these needs and helps you identify anything that might threaten their provision. The root chakra is also responsible for the fight-or-flight response, which we activate when we feel threatened.

As stated earlier, the root chakra is the foundation for the other chakras and therefore was the first to appear when we entered this world. When a baby is born, it first gains a primal instinct for survival, and using the sense of smell and its mouth, the baby will try to sense the world around it and find food. The baby turns its head towards the stimulus it is sensing and makes sucking motions with its mouth as it attempts to find food. This primitive process, known as **rooting**, is driven by the root chakra. With time, as it caters to its primal need for food and survival, the baby will stop sensing around for food and instead move directly to the object that provides the food, whether that is its mother's breast or a feeding bottle. This acts as an affirmation to the baby that the world will support its survival and helps the baby form a connection to those supporting its survival and the rest of the world.

The root chakra acts as a link between our bodies' energy and the energy fields within the physical world. It provides us with the motivation to do the actions necessary for our survival, such as eating, sleeping, and procreating. The root chakra also helps us to form a sense of belonging within our environment and to develop our self-esteem and personal integrity. It has an influence on our youthfulness, creativity, passion. In addition, the root chakra gives us the confidence and resourcefulness we need to get through life even when faced with challenging situations.

Signs of an Aligned Root Chakra

You can tell when your root chakra (and all other chakras) align by looking at your life, your behaviors, and your physical wellbeing. A well-aligned and balanced root chakra makes us feel safe, fearless, determined in pursuing our goals, feeling at home in the world, and it also increases our sense of self-worth and self-confidence. Some signs of a well-aligned root chakra and free-flowing energy include:

Increased Passion and Vitality: When your root chakra aligns well, you become a lot more passionate about whatever activities you engage in, whether that is in your work, your hobbies, or any other responsibilities. You also become more passionate about your friends and family.

A Sense of Ease: A balanced root chakra allows energy to flow freely, which allows the other things in your life to flow smoothly too. You feel that the universe is meeting your every need. You can finally do things that before proved difficult now with less effort. Every aspect of your life—from your relationships to your career and finances—starts to go well.

Fearlessness: An aligned root chakra makes you feel connected to the Earth and gives you the feeling that the universe will provide everything you need. This connection also makes you confident in your ability to handle whatever challenges life throws at you. As a result, any worries and fears that plagued you previously become a thing of the past. You stop worrying about the future and instead start embracing the spirit of adventure the future holds, knowing well that you will be in control regardless of whatever happens.

Increased Sexual Drive: Remember, the root chakra controls your instincts for sex and survival. An aligned root chakra increases your overall sense of safety and security, which increases your desire for sex. This trait is embedded deep in our mammalian traits. Out in the wild, sex, reproduction, and raising offspring makes animals vulnerable to threats from other animals. Therefore, most mammals evolved an in-built mechanism that *reduces* sexual drive whenever they are in a dangerous environment. Even if we no longer live in the jungle, the same thing applies to us today. This evolution directly links our libido to our sense of safety.

Financial Abundance: There's a common saying that states that *all the money you will ever make in this world is inside your mind*. While this is a modern saying, ancient Hindus also believed in something similar: the universe has an abundance of energy accessible to everyone in the world. Your material and financial abundance depend on your ability to access and manifest this energy. When your root chakra is balanced, it allows the free flow of energy between you and the universe, making it easier for you to manifest this energy to achieve financial abundance. You will become more confident in yourself and your abilities, and you will have no fear of going after your goals and dreams, all of which contribute toward this financial abundance.

Healthy Weight: As we saw earlier, the root chakra influences the function of the adrenal glands, among many other body organs. The role of the adrenal organs is to produce cortisol. A well-aligned root chakra improves the regulation of cortisol levels within your body, which increases your metabolism and reduces stress. The increased metabolism and reduced stress can help you attain a healthy weight level without having to make any other major changes to your lifestyle.

Reduced Attachment: The root chakra influences your sense of safety, belonging, and self-identity. If your root chakra is not well-balanced, you won't feel safe and confident in your self-identity, and therefore you will look for safety and self-identity in your career, social status, material things, and so on. This leads to an excessive attachment to whatever object helps you find safety and self-identity. As your root chakra becomes aligned, however, you will feel more secure and become confident in your self-identity, resulting in a reduced attachment to the objects that previously provided you with safety since they are no longer necessary.

Other signs of a well-aligned root chakra include increased satisfaction with your life, increased satisfaction with your job/career, improved sense of wellbeing, prosperity, and improved health.

Signs of an Unbalanced Root Chakra

Often, we find that our root chakra is not well-aligned, which can lead to several problems in our physical, mental, and emotional wellbeing. Question is, how do you know when your root chakra is unbalanced? Some signs of an unbalanced root chakra include:

Feelings of Insecurity: When your root chakra is blocked, energy will not flow freely, you will not feel connected to the Earth, and you will not have confidence in your self-identity, leading to feelings of insecurity. If you doubt yourself or worry endlessly about your health and safety, these are signs that your root chakra is unbalanced. Here, it's not about fleeting feelings of insecurity that appear for a short time before subsiding, as it's normal to worry and feel insecure sometimes. For instance, if you are driving and the person behind you is driving recklessly, you might worry about your safety. Similarly, if you are about to go for a big interview, you might have some doubts about yourself. This is perfectly normal and doesn't mean that your root chakra is unbalanced. However, if you realize these feelings of doubt and insecurity are constantly on your mind, it is a clear sign that you need to align your root chakra.

Obsession With Money: People who have a poorly balanced root chakra are not confident in the universe's ability to provide their needs. They are afraid that they will reach a point when their survival on Earth will not be supported. This fear manifests itself through an obsession with money. You are someone who constantly worries that they do not have enough money has a constant fear that they could become broke one day. You work way too much to ease your anxiety about money; you are thrifty, and it triggers you when your spouse or someone close to you spends what you think is too much money.

Greed: Besides making you obsessed with money, the lack of confidence in the universe's ability to meet your needs also leads to greed. Since you are afraid that you might lack in the future, you try to make up for it by consuming/hoarding as much as you can today, even when doing so comes at the expense of others. You will also find it hard to share what you have with others because you think you will not regain that which you have shared out to others.

Lack of Trust: An unbalanced root chakra can also make it difficult for you to place your trust in others. You view every interaction with other people with suspicion and believe that everyone has some ulterior motive that you need to watch out for. You may also disconnect yourself from others and find it harder to ask others for help (even if you need it).

Low Self-Confidence: An unbalanced root chakra also leads to low self-confidence. You think you are inadequate and find it difficult to show your authentic self to others, especially around strangers. Instead, you put on a pretentious self that you think other people are more likely to love. You might also feel you are an impostor and you don't deserve what you have in your life. A lack of connection to your foundation can cause this lack of confidence.

Fearfulness: The lack of connection to your foundation because of an unbalanced root chakra also leads to fearfulness. Instead of making informed decisions based on a logical analysis of facts, you make rash decisions driven purely by fear. Instead of making choices guided by what you want to achieve in life, you make choices prompted by something you want to avoid.

Sexual Dysfunction: As we saw earlier, the sexual desire for most mammals—humans included—diminishes when they are in an environment that does not feel safe for them. Since an unbalanced root chakra makes you feel unsafe and insecure, this can lead to a decreased desire for sex or even complete sexual dysfunction.

Physical Symptoms: Some physical problems of a blocked or unbalanced root chakra can occur in your digestion, the large intestines, the bladder, the legs and feet, and the lower back. Other problems such as infections, poor circulation, cramps, swelling, inflammation, fatigue, weight gain in the lower body (around the waist and thighs), prostate problems in men, eating disorders, restlessness and a racing heartbeat, and cold temperatures in the extremities (hands and feet).

Some other signs and symptoms associated with a blocked or unbalanced root chakra include depression and depressive symptoms, anger issues, panic, worry and frustration, overthinking, negativity and cynicism, lack of concentration, nightmares, disorganization, too much reliance on external feedback, and trouble making decisions.

Techniques to Align Your Root Chakra

Keeping the root chakra balanced is important because it acts as the foundation for the other six chakras. Unfortunately, the root chakra is also one of the most unbalanced chakras for most people, and almost everyone has had their root chakra blocked or unbalanced. Some have never even had a perfectly aligned root chakra throughout their lives. Sometimes, the blockage stems from that which happened to you during your childhood, while in other situations, occurrences that resulted in your feeling unsafe or ungrounded or circumstances in your recent past could have caused the blockage.

If you are feeling unsafe or ungrounded, or if you are experiencing several of the signs and symptoms covered above, you need to bring your root chakra back into alignment. Question is, how do you do it? We will look at some techniques you can use to align your root chakra.

Identify the Problem

The first step to aligning your root chakra is to identify the areas of your life that are getting affected by the blockage and unbalancing of the root chakra. In what areas of your life do you feel threatened or insecure? In what areas of your life do you doubt yourself or feel like an impostor? In what areas of your life do you feel disconnected from reality? In what areas of your life do you feel your confidence is lacking? Identifying the areas of your life that are being impacted by the unbalanced root chakra is an important part of resolving the issue. If you skip this first step, it will be a lot harder to align your root chakra, even if you follow all the other techniques described below.

Root Chakra Meditation

Meditation is one of the best ways of healing your body and unblocking your chakras. Remember, we saw that some ancient traditions even used chakras as meditation guides; therefore, using the chakras in meditation is an effective way of aligning them. If you have had prior experience with meditation, chakra meditation will be easy because it is similar to regular meditation. The only difference is that **chakra meditation** focuses specifically on the area of your body where you can locate that specific chakra. Below is a simple routine you can use for **root chakra meditation**.

- Find a comfortable place and sit upright, making sure that your spine is straight. Push your shoulders

back (without drooping). Make sure you relax your muscles and can sit in this position for a while without feeling uncomfortable.
- Close your eyes and take a deep breath. You want to breathe in through the nose as deep as possible and then breathe out through your mouth. Repeat these breathing movements.
- As you continue breathing deeply, focus on the area around just below your tailbone near the perineum; this is where you locate the root chakra. Focus on what you are feeling in this area and note any tightness you might be having here.
- In your mind, imagine the color red (the color of the root chakra) glowing in your root chakra. Pay attention to the red glow and see it slowly growing in size and expanding outwards. Feel your body become warm and relaxed as the red glow expands. Remain in this state for three to five minutes.
- Think about yourself as a mountain and that you are strong and sturdy while you breathe in and out.
- Slowly let go of the image of the red glow and return your focus back to your breathing.
- After about five breaths, open your eyes slowly and allow them to adjust to the light in the room. Remain seated for a few minutes until all your focus is back in the room.

Your root chakra meditation technique is now complete.

Yoga Techniques

Yoga is also another good way of healing your body, and there are some yoga techniques that will help you unblock and realign your root chakra. The following are some good yoga techniques to try for this purpose.

Standing Forward Fold: Also referred to as **Uttanasana**, this is a simple pose that involves standing upright, with your spine straight, and then bending down at the hips until your fingertips or palms touch the mat. Alternatively, you can place your palms just behind your ankles. Allow your head to hang and try to relax as much as possible while holding this position.

The standing forward pose stretches your hips, hamstrings, and legs, while at the same time strengthening the knees. This allows the root chakra to open up and at the same time enables stable grounding.

Garland Pose: We also know this pose as **Malasana**. To get into this pose, start by standing upright. Set your feet shoulder-width apart and point your toes outward. Hold your hands in front of your chest in the prayer position and then bend your knees, going down until your hips are as close to the ground as possible. You should also ensure that your knees are directly above your toes and facing the same direction. Hold this position for a few minutes. If you find it hard to hold the position, you can have a blanket or a block under your tailbone to support you.

The garland pose strengthens your ankles, calves, and lower back while opening up your hips and bringing you closer to the Earth, all of which help you unblock your root chakra. As you hold this position, picture yourself connected to the Earth and channeling the Earth's energy into yourself.

Head-to-Knee Forward Bend: This yoga pose is also referred to as **Janu Sirsasana**. To get into this pose, start by sitting upright with your legs stretched out straight in front of you. Fold your left knee and bring the ball of your left foot as close to your groin as possible. Keeping your spine long, bend at the hips and above your outstretched right leg.

Try to bring your head as close as possible to your right knee. Keep your spine as straight as you can while doing this pose.

The head-to-knee forward bend pose helps make you feel grounded and improves your flexibility in the hips, hamstrings, and lower back. It also stimulates the functioning of the liver and kidney and enhances the flow of energy through the root chakra.

Grounding

The root chakra is all about your connection to the Earth; therefore, when your root chakra is not well-aligned or blocked, you are not connecting yourself to the ground. However, you can open your root chakra by performing a **simple grounding exercise**. Below are the steps on how to perform the exercise.

- Stand upright with your body relaxed and your feet firmly planted on the ground (preferably barefooted).
- Spread your feet so they are directly below your shoulders.
- Bend your knees slightly while pushing your pelvis forward.
- Sink your weight downwards while maintaining your balance by ensuring that your weight distributed evenly over the soles of your feet.
- Hold that position for a few minutes.

Form an Intimate Connection With the Earth

Since the root chakra is about your connection to the Earth, connecting intimately with the Earth is an important part of healing it. There are a few ways to connect with the Earth; one simple method is to go outside to your garden and walk barefoot. Focus on the contact your feet make with the ground. Going for walks, hikes, and climbs and spending time with nature are all great ways to form a connection with the Earth. You can also connect with the Earth by planting trees with your own hands.

Alternatively, you can use visualization to build an intimate connection with the Earth. To do this, close your eyes and imagine a red-colored cord running from the center of the Earth to your root chakra.

Use Root Chakra Affirmations

Affirmations and mantras are great for reprogramming your thinking patterns, and they can be very useful in helping you heal your root chakra. As with all other kinds of affirmations and mantras, root chakra affirmations will be most effective when you repeat them regularly. Make it a habit to recite these mantras every morning when you wake, before going to sleep, or immediately after you finish root chakra meditation. You could also print them out and place them in a prominent place where you can see them and recite them as you go through your day. These include places such as the bathroom mirror, the fridge, or even on your desk at work.

You can also make these affirmations a part of your root chakra yoga practice, repeating the mantras while in the yoga poses discussed above. You can also make the root chakra affirmations more effective by holding one of the root chakra stones while reciting the mantras.

Some root chakra affirmations you could consider include:

- I am safe and secure.
- I am grounded.
- I am home.
- I have everything I need to survive.
- My body is my home.
- I am connected to and supported by the Earth.
- I am connected to my body.
- I love myself.
- I am fearless.
- I am strong.
- I am at peace.
- I feel centered.

Use Root Chakra Stones

Each chakra is associated with some special, **precious stones**, many of which come in the form of jewelry. Holding these stones or wearing them can be effective in realigning an imbalanced or blocked chakra. You can also use the stones in your yoga sessions or when reciting your chakra affirmations.

Some special stones that can help you realign your root chakra include:

- **Red Jasper:** As the name implies, this stone shares the same color associated with the root chakra (red). The red jasper symbolizes **balance** and is therefore useful for those who have erratic mood swings.

- **Red Carnelian:** This stone is also pale red, along with orange hues running in interesting patterns across the stone. The red carnelian is linked to feelings of **bravery** and **strength**. This stone is ideal for those who constantly feel afraid and have a hard time stepping outside their comfort zone.

- **Obsidian**: Unlike the other two stones, obsidian does not share the same color scheme; it is instead black. Obsidian associates with **protection** and can make you feel more secure in your life.

Engage in Physical Activity

Being physically active is also great for aligning and balancing your root chakra. Remember, the root chakra is all about your physical self. Therefore, if you feel that your root chakra is unbalanced, get in the habit of engaging in physical activities that involve a lot of movement, especially with your legs and feet.

When people think about engaging in physical activity, most think about working out in the gym. However, if working out in the gym is not your cup of tea, there are many other ways of engaging in physical activity, such as taking part in a physical sport you enjoy, going on walks every day, engaging in martial arts, dancing, and even just doing household chores such as mowing the lawn or vacuuming. Activities that increase your adrenaline, such as bungee jumping, skydiving, and zip-lining are also great for stimulating your root chakra.

Another great way to inspire the root chakra is to exercise the perineum, which is the area between your groin and the anus. To exercise the perineum, try contracting the perineum muscle as you breathe in and then allow the muscle to relax as you breathe out. Repeat this process for about three to five minutes. This is a simple exercise that you can do just about anywhere, whether you are sitting in traffic, watching TV, working at your office desk, standing, or even as you take a walk down the street.

Add More Red Into Your Life

Like we saw earlier, the color red represents the root chakra; therefore, adding more red into your life can also help to realign this chakra. Adding red to your life is straightforward, and you can do it by wearing more red-colored clothing, adding red pieces of décor in your home, having red curtains or pillows, or having a red notebook on your work desk. Doing anything that will allow you to see the color red more often can help you realign your root chakra.

Use Aromatherapy Healing

Aromatherapy is great for realigning the root chakra because it gives you a connection to your surroundings. For instance, if you went to a foul-smelling place, you will probably have trouble concentrating on anything else because your sense of smell constantly reminds you of your surroundings. The sense of smell also gives us a sense of belonging and rekindles old memories. For instance, encountering a smell you associate with the bed you slept in as a child will bring back memories from your childhood and create a connection to your childhood home.

When trying to realign your root chakra using aromatherapy, go for flower and Earthy scents. Some great scents for realigning your root chakra include Ylang Ylang, sandalwood, myrrh, rosemary, and patchouli.

Things That Cause Imbalances in Your Root Chakra

Having seen various ways through which you can realign an imbalanced or blocked root chakra, it is also good to know about some things that may cause your root chakra to become *blocked* or *imbalanced*. In most cases, blockage or imbalance of the root chakra is caused by things that threaten your sense of security. These include:

- Childhood abuse
- Toxic relationships
- Abandonment by a loved one
- Longtime illness or bad news regarding health
- Poverty or encountering financial difficulties
- Job loss or threatened with
- Heartbreak
- Conflict with close family members
- Rejection
- Traumatic events

Aside from that which can threaten your sense of security, other things that can take your root chakra out of alignment include:

- Too much television
- Excessive Internet use
- Loss of touch with family and friends
- Too much time indoors

- Overuse of alcohol and drugs
- Overdependence on family and friends.

As I end this chapter, I want you to note that all seven chakras are interconnected. Changes in one chakra will usually impact the other chakras, which is especially true for the root chakra because it provides a foundation for all the others. Therefore, before trying to balance the other chakras, make sure that your root chakra is aligned. With an imbalanced root chakra, it is next to impossible to balance the others properly because the foundation from the root chakra will be lacking.

CHAPTER THREE: THE SACRAL CHAKRA

The sacral chakra, or **Svadhisthana**, is the second chakra in the seven chakra system. The term Svadhisthana is a Sanskrit word meaning "one's own place." This term is used to refer to the sacral chakra since this is the chakra that allows you to express your real self. The term Svadhisthana can also mean "sweetness," regarding the sexual and sensual pleasure of life.

We associate the sacral chakra with emotional response, creativity, and sensuality, as well as relationships, sexuality, reproduction, flow, and care. Because of this, it is considered as the seat of a person's emotions.

The principle of pleasure drives this chakra. The sacral chakra guides us in pursuing happiness, joy, and loving relationships. The element of the sacral chakra is **water**, which is an illustration of the fluidity and flow of this chakra.

Besides holding our feelings, emotions, and desires, the sacral chakra also hides our dark side or our "shadow." The **shadow** refers to all the things about ourselves that we dislike. While we try to keep these dark sides of our lives repressed, we cannot eliminate them completely, and they find ways of manifesting themselves in our lives now and then. This dark side contributes to things such as faulty relationships.

We can locate the sacral chakra about two fingers above your coccyx or tailbone, or about two to three inches below your navel, at the same level as the sacrum (hence the name *sacral chakra*). The location of the sacral chakra is just above the root chakra, which provides the sacral chakra with the nurturing energy from the Earth.

In the body, the sacral chakra is associated with the sexual glands, uterus, testes and ovaries, prostate, bowels, kidneys, pelvis, lumbar region, bodily fluids, and the circulatory system.

The sacral chakra is represented by the color **orange** because it is the color of joy, creativity, sexuality, and enthusiasm. Being a combination of the happiness of yellow and the energy of red, orange also represents self-assuredness, independence, confidence, fascination, attraction, encouragement, and stimulation.

Orange can also symbolize self-respect and success. It illustrates the freedom to be ourselves and to follow activities and interests that give us joy. It is a color that makes us social and independent while allowing us to stimulate our emotions and allow us to get rid of our inhibitions.

Sometimes, the sacral chakra may also represented by the color white or a very light blue, though is very rare. These colors are a representation of water, which is the element of this chakra.

The symbol for the sacral chakra is a circle (lotus flower)

with six petals, with the shape of a moon crescent inside the lotus flower. All of these elements have their own distinct meanings.

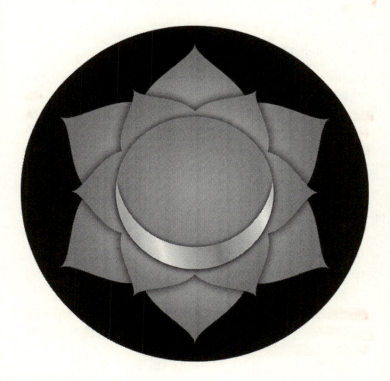

The Circle

The circle in the sacral chakra symbol represents the cyclic nature of life where all living things go through birth, death, and rebirth. The circle is also used to symbolize water, the element of the sacral chakra.

The Six Petals of the Lotus Flower

The six petals around the lotus flower represent the six emotions that every person must conquer to purify their Svadhisthana. These six emotions are desire, pride, anger, hatred, jealousy, and cruelty.

The Crescent Moon

The crescent moon on the symbol signifies the connection between the energy of water and that of the moon. The phases of the moon usually influence the fluctuations and the waves in the water (*oceans*). Similarly, fluctuations in the sacral chakra sway our emotions. The moon is a representation of the association of the sacral chakra with sexuality and procreation. The moon takes about 28 days to go through all its phases, which is the same number of days needed for women to complete the menstrual cycle. Some Hindu traditions also believe that the crescent moon is a portrayal of constant movement and the never-ending cycle of change.

The sacral chakra is closely linked to our personal identity and how we relate to and respond to the seductive forces that are part of our external world. Without a well-balanced sacral chakra, we don't have the strength to have healthy responses to these seductive forces, something that can easily lead to addictions to sex, drugs, money, and gambling. A well-balanced sacral chakra allows us to develop a healthy ego and makes it possible for us to interact with the external world without losing ourselves. If you have a healthy sacral chakra, you can control your desires and you can be confident in who you are.

The sacral chakra is also responsible for helping us form deep, healthy connections to other people and is responsible for sexual attraction. It is what *turns us on*. It also influences the things that bring us joy. Whatever hobby you enjoy—be it fishing, painting, singing, or dancing, for example—it is the sacral chakra that allows you to find enjoyment in that activity.

Being closely connected to procreation, the sacral chakra is also responsible for making us creative. It allows us to give birth to new things, whether the new thing is a project you have always had in mind, a new painting, a friendship with someone you just met, a new dance move, or even a relationship with someone you fancy. The sacral chakra also inhibits our fears and boundaries and allows us to go after our creative pursuits and the things that bring us happiness.

Indicators of an Open and Aligned Sacral Chakra

Since the sacral chakra is the seat of your emotions, a well-aligned sacral chakra will cause a healthy relationship with your emotions. You will feel emotionally stable, intuitive, energized, and compassionate. It will be easy to relate with other people as emotions play a key role in our relationships with others; your creativity will be on high gear, and you will have a healthy and fulfilling sexual life. You will find beauty and great sensory experiences all around you.

When your sacral chakra is open, you will become more creative, passionate, sensual, with a feeling of being present in your body and connected to your feelings and emotions. It will also fill you with joy most of the time.

Blockage and Imbalance of the Sacral Chakra

We have already seen that our feelings, emotions, and desires are stored within the energy of the sacral chakra. Unfortunately, we live in a society that encourages people to keep a tight lid on their emotions and not express themselves fully. I want you to think about your childhood for a moment. How many times were you told not to cry? How many times did you talk about something you wanted and people told you it was not appropriate? In adolescence, how many times were you told that expressing your sexuality is shameful? With such influences, most of us internalize the idea that we should suppress our emotions and desires, and unfortunately, these suppressed emotions and desires remain stuck in our sacral chakra and cause it to get blocked.

Aside from these suppressed emotions, blockages of the sacral chakra can also be caused by things that affect your sexuality or your creativity. Some examples include getting rejected by a potential lover, being sexually incompatible with someone you are in a relationship with, reproductive health problems, and having your creative outputs rejected, such as when you come up with something like a novel, a painting, a song or a business, only to have the people around you reject it.

Once our sacral chakra becomes blocked and misaligned, we lose our ability to form healthy bonds with others; we experience emotional instability; we get into addictions; we become depressed; we become impassionate and lose our desire for sex, and we become afraid of change and become critical of ourselves.

The following are some common signs and symptoms associated with a blocked or misaligned sacral chakra.

Negative And Destructive Emotions

Do you often have to deal with emotions such as rage and anger? Have you felt envious or jealous of others? Do you overreact whenever someone states opinions contrary to yours? Do you feel intense frustration when the slightest thing does not go your way? All these emotions are destructive and detrimental to your wellbeing, and they could be an indicator you have a blocked or imbalanced sacral chakra.

Addictions and Uncontrolled Indulgence

The sacral chakra influences our desires and controls our responses to these desires. In situations where our sacral chakra is excessively open, someone might have very strong desires and very little control over these desires. This manifests itself through addictions and overindulgence. Such a passion will easily get addicted to things such as sex, drugs, gambling money, and food. These desires hardly get satisfied because the sacral chakra is excessively open.

Lost in Fantasies

People who have an unbalanced sacral chakra have a reduced ability to enjoy the pleasures of life; therefore, they try to experience these pleasures by fantasizing about them. For instance, instead of going out, meeting potential sexual partners, connecting, and enjoying one's sexuality with them, a person with a blocked sacral chakra will instead lose themselves in sexual fantasies.

Lack of Fulfillment

This one closely relates to the previous point. As the sacral chakra is in charge of our desires, someone who has a healthy sacral chakra knows how to feel fulfilled or satisfied. However, for someone who has an imbalanced root chakra, they will hardly have any sense of fulfillment, regardless of what they do. Such a person constantly feels like they are lacking something in their lives, and try as much as they can, this feeling will never go away until they heal their sacral chakra.

Overdependence on Others

The sacral chakra influences how we form relationships with other people. When your sacral chakra is healthy and balanced, you are comfortable in your skin and can form balanced relationships with others. When your sacral chakra is unbalanced, however, your relationships are also unbalanced, and you may become too dependent on other people. If you become too codependent on the people in your life and feeling like you cannot survive without them, this could be a sign that your sacral chakra is off-kilter.

Reduced or Excessive Libido

The sacral chakra controls your sexual urges and influences your sexual attraction to other people. When the sacral chakra is blocked, you may experience a *reduced* desire for sex. If your sacral chakra is excessively open, it might cause an *increased* desire for sex, possibly leading to a person trying to have sexual relations with every attractive person they come across.

Physical Symptoms

A blocked or misaligned sacral chakra can also affect your physical health and wellbeing. Some physical symptoms of a blocked or imbalanced sacral chakra include testicular and prostate diseases, ovarian cysts, endometriosis, miscarriages, ectopic pregnancies, infertility, muscle tension and abdominal cramps, bladder and urinary tract infections, and an irregular menstrual cycle.

Besides the above signs, there are several other symptoms that may signal a blocked or unbalanced sacral chakra. These include:

- Being controlled by emotions; inability to keep emotions in check; emotional confusion
- Lack of passion, joy, and happiness; emotionless
- Stuck in one mood or feeling; anxiety
- Decreased self-esteem and self-confidence
- Reduced creativity
- Trouble connecting and associating with other people; repetitive dysfunctional relationships
- Inability to deal with changes in life
- Feeling unimportant, unloved, and unaccepted
- Self-sabotage and fear of happiness

Ways to Heal the Sacral Chakra

We have already seen that having a blocked or unbalanced chakra can lead to physical and emotional problems and affect your ability to connect with and form relationships with other people. So, what are you supposed to do if you notice signs signaling that your sacral chakra is out of alignment? The next sections outline steps for healing your sacral chakra.

Identify the Problem

The first step to healing your sacral chakra is to identify how the misalignment of the sacral chakra is affecting you. Identifying how this misalignment affects you requires self-inquiry and introspection. Only by understanding your emotions and reactions can you identify the problem you have in your life and then work on healing yourself. Some questions you should ask yourself here include:

- Do I consider myself attractive?
- Am I confident in myself and my self-image, or do I often doubt myself?
- What things do I find attractive? What things do I hate? How do these things affect my life?
- Are there moments that I feel like my emotions are running my life?
- Am I moderate in my enjoyment of life's little pleasures, or do I go overboard and indulge excessively?
- Am I obsessed with pursuing pleasure?
- Are there areas of my life where I feel like I am not connected to myself?
- Do I feel connected to my sexuality?
- Do I take responsibility for my pleasure and my wellbeing?
- How is my sexual life? Am I satisfied?
- Are all my desires being met?
- Are there areas of my life where I feel like my emotions are being suppressed?
- Are there emotions and feelings that I am having trouble letting go?

- Do I enjoy my relationships with others? How intimate are my relationships with my partners?
- Does my life feel alive or dull?

Answering these questions will help you recognize ways through which your sacral chakra is affecting your life, which will be useful in helping you heal and align your sacral chakra. For instance, if you realize that your current sexual life doesn't satisfy you, you can put more focus on finding ways through which you can express your sexuality and satisfy your desires.

Meditation

Like with the root chakra, meditation is one of the most effective ways to align an unbalanced sacral chakra. Meditation for this chakra is like standard meditation practices, though it involves an element of visualization that is not part of model practices. Below are the steps to follow for sacral chakra meditation:

- Find a comfortable, quiet place where you are likely to be undisturbed for the duration of your meditation session. It is also advisable to wear loose-fitting, comfortable clothes. If possible, dim the lights if they are too bright.
- Sit in a position that will allow you to remain comfortable for the duration of your meditation session. Keep your back straight, push your shoulders back, and relax your limbs.
- Close our eyes and then slowly take several deep breaths, inhaling through the nose, holding the

breath for a few seconds and then exhaling slowly through the mouth.
- After repeating your breaths a few times, focus your attention on the area below your navel where you can locate your sacral chakra.
- Visualize an orange circle spinning in the location of your sacral chakra. Visualize an orange light emanating from this spinning circle and spreading throughout your body in rippling waves. Feel the sensation of your body warming to match the spreading of this orange light.
- Hold the image in your mind for about five minutes, and then slowly let go of the image of the orange light and return your focus back to your breathing.
- After five breaths, open your eyes slowly and allow them to adjust to the light in the room. Remain seated for a few minutes until all your focus is back in the room.

Use Hip-Opening Yoga Postures

Yoga postures are also useful for healing unbalanced chakras. When your sacral chakra is out of alignment, a lot of the emotional and physical tension resulting from this lack of alignment is stored in the area around the hips. Imagine a time you found yourself in a stressful situation or watch your body the next time you are in a stressful situation; you will realize that you have a lot of tension in your lower abdomen and the area around your hips.

Therefore, to heal the sacral chakra, you need to focus on yoga poses that help to open up your hips. The following are some hip-opening yoga poses to unblock your sacral chakra.

Wide-Angle Seated Forward Bend: Also referred to as the **Upavistha Konasana**, this pose opens up the sacral chakra and strengthens your spine while stimulating the organs around the lower abdomen.

One-Legged King Pigeon Pose: This is a seated, back-bending yoga pose which is a variation of the more popular pigeon pose, also referred to as **Eka pada rajakapotasana**. This yoga pose is great for opening up the hips and allowing the flow of energy through the sacral chakra while stretching the shoulders and chest and stimulating the organs in your abdomen.

Bound Angle Pose: Also known as **Baddha Konasana**, this posture opens up the sacral chakra and dissipates energy imbalance while stimulating the organs in your lower abdomen.

Sacral Chakra Affirmations

We already saw that affirmations and mantras are a great way to heal and realign blocked and unbalanced chakras, and this includes the sacral chakra. However, the affirmations used to heal and realign the sacral chakra differ from those used to heal and realign the root chakra, since each of these chakras relates to different behaviors and traits. Some affirmations and mantras you can use to unblock the sacral chakra include:

- I am a strong creative person who loves her creations and am full of inspiration.
- I am deserving of life's pleasures and having my needs met.
- I am confident in my sexuality.
- It is safe for me to express my sexuality in healthy, creative, and fun ways.
- I am confident in myself and everything I offer to the world.
- I am comfortable inside my body.
- I can attract and maintain great relationships with good, loving people.
- I experience joy and satisfaction every day.
- I can go through life's changes and come out unscathed.

You can recite these affirmations first thing when you wake up in the morning, every night before you go to sleep, or whenever you find yourself in any situation that could block your sacral chakra.

Eating Foods That Heal the Sacral Chakra

Changing your diet also has an influence on your chakras and can help unblock or realign an unbalanced chakra. There are several foods that can help cleanse and heal the sacral chakra, including:

- **Broths and Teas**: Liquids are great for cleansing the sacral chakra; therefore, including teas and tasty vegetable broths in your diet can work wonders for your second chakra.
- **Oranges**: Considering that the sacral chakra is represented by the color orange, it is not surprising that oranges are a great option for cleansing the sacral chakra. Besides oranges, other fleshy orange-colored fruits like peaches, mangoes, and papayas are also great for bringing your sacral chakra back into alignment.
- **Coconuts**: These tropical fruits are full of healthy fats and oils, good for your heart. They contain a lot of energy and can help get you in the right mood for creativity. Because of this, they are a great option for those who have trouble with their sacral chakra.
- **Seeds**: Many kinds of seeds are great for activating and healing the sacral area. Some that are particularly good at this include hemp, poppy, pumpkin, and sunflower seeds.

Sacral Chakra Healing Stones

We already saw that some gemstones associate with each chakra, which can be useful in healing their related chakra. Some healing stones that can help you realign your sacral chakra include:

- **Orange Calcite:** Considering that orange is the color of the sacral chakra, it is not surprising that this orange stone can help realign the sacral chakra. Users suggest this stone to be good at **reuniting the body** and **mind**, **enhancing creativity**, and helping you **overcome emotional barriers**.

- **Carnelian**: While it comes in various shades, the carnelian is usually a reddish-brown. Note that this is a different stone from the *red carnelian*, which is used to heal the root chakra. Also referred to as the **singer's stone**, carnelian helps you unlock your **artistry** and **creativity**.

- **Moonstone**: This is another stone available in multiple colors; however, the most effective for healing the sacral chakra is the **peach moonstone**. They say the peach moonstone is great at channeling **loving energy** and **stimulating the mind**.

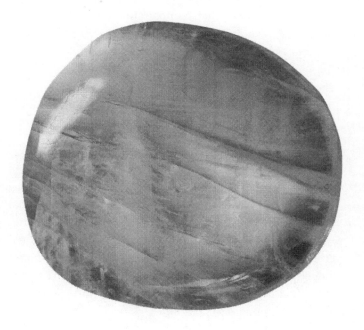

There are various ways of using the above stones to heal your sacral chakra. One option is to wear the stones on your body as a way of optimizing energy flow. You can do this by having the stones made into jewelry such as a bracelet, a ring, or a pendant on a necklace.

Alternatively, you can hold the stones in your hands and allow them to transfer their energy to your body. This is especially effective when you hold them when you are meditating or during your yoga sessions. You also have the option of placing the stones on your lower abdomen in the location of your sacral chakra. Similar to using the stones during meditation or yoga, placing them on the lumbar area is also an effective way of healing your sacral chakra.

It is good to note that discovering the particular stone or a combination of stones that is most effective for you might take some time, so don't get discouraged if you don't notice any effects the first few times you use the stones. As you continue practicing with the stones, you will gradually identify those that work best for you.

Aromatherapy for Sacral Chakra Healing

Aromatherapy is another effective yet simple way of unblocking and realigning the sacral chakra. Aromatherapy is basically all about using essential oils with aromas that promote the healing of the sacral chakra. You can either apply the essential oils on your body (in the area around the lower abdomen), use them together with sacral chakra healing stones, or use them during meditation. Some scents that are great or healing the sacral chakra include patchouli, sandalwood, rose, orange, and Ylang Ylang.

Connect With Water

Considering that water is the element that represents the sacral chakra, connecting with water is also great for healing. The greatest way to connect with water is to spend some time relaxing near an open body of water—an ocean, a lake, a river, or a stream. Wading through or dangling your feet in the body of water will allow energy to flow more effectively between your body and the water. If you are nowhere near a body of water, taking a shower or warm bath can also help you connect with water.

Dance

Dancing is one of the simplest and most entertaining ways of healing and aligning your sacral chakra. The fluidity of your body while dancing in response to the rhythm of the music can help trigger the flow of blocked energies. Therefore, if you feel that your sacral chakra is blocked, it might be time to turn on some music and dance like no one's watching.

Give Up Toxic Relationships

Remember, being in a toxic relationship is one way through which your sacral chakra gets blocked. Therefore, if you find yourself in toxic relationships that bring you frustration, do not support you at all, or do not promote your growth, you need to get out of these relationships. If you don't want to cut off the relationship, then you need to focus on resolving whatever issues are making the relationships toxic.

Engage in Creative Pursuits

We have already seen that the sacral chakra is associated with your creativity and passion. This means that you can trigger the flow of energy in the sacral chakra by engaging in any activities that allow you to unleash your creativity. Whenever you have the time, engage in any hobbies that allow your creative energies to flow. This can include drawing, painting, dancing, writing, design, or any other creative pursuit.

Engage in Sensual Sex

Considering that the sacral chakra links closely with your sexuality and pursuit of sensual pleasures, engaging in sensual sex can also trigger the flow of energy in a blocked sacral chakra. Here, the key is to make love with lots of tenderness, intimacy, and attention to your partner. You want to feel deeply connected to your partner, rather than just having sex for the sake of getting off. If you don't have a partner, you can still find the energies around your sacral chakra flowing by engaging in sensual self-pleasuring and masturbation. Once again, remember that the point here is not to get yourself off. Instead, you should be gentle and tender, and put all the focus on the sensations coursing through your body as you masturbate. Even if you don't end up with an orgasm, you will still have triggered the flow of sacral chakra energies.

Other ways to heal your sacral chakra include taking part in activities such as Tai Chi and Qi-Gong, ensuring that you are getting enough sleep, being patient and understanding with yourself rather than berating yourself for every wrong thing you do, drinking lots of fluids, engaging in sensual activities such as baths and massages, and listening to sounds in the 417 Hz frequency.

CHAPTER FOUR: THE SOLAR PLEXUS CHAKRA

The third chakra is the solar plexus chakra, also known as **Manipura** in Sanskrit. The name *Manipura* means "shining gem." The solar plexus chakra is at the core of a person's identity, personality, and ego, and is responsible for the formation of the independent self—who you are with no connection to your tribe or any external relationships. A well-aligned solar plexus chakra allows you to exhibit your authentic self with confidence. It allows your personality to shine, hence the reference to the shining gem.

The solar plexus chakra gives you an integrated sense of who you are as a person. It is the source of your confidence and the center of your personal power and will. It allows you to overcome your fears, take responsibility for your life, and make the right choices towards pursuing your true path and the life you envision for yourself.

Like you might have guessed from the name, we locate the solar plexus chakra around the solar plexus. This is the area in the upper section of your belly, just below your diaphragm, or the area between the lower part of the chest and the navel. This is the area that feels hollow between your ribs, just below your chest. The solar plexus chakra influences the function of organs such as the adrenal glands, pancreas, muscles, and the digestive system.

The color **yellow** is used to represent the solar plexus chakra and is the color of **fire**, the element of this chakra. Yellow represents the fire that burns within you and gives you the power and confidence to assert yourself and show your brilliance to the world. The color yellow is a representation of the brightness that you radiate out to the world when you have a well-balanced solar plexus chakra. Yellow associates with traits such as optimism, vibrancy, intellect, and energy. It also relates to youth and new beginnings.

The symbol for the solar plexus chakra is a yellow lotus flower with ten petals. In the middle of the lotus flower is a downward-pointing triangle, which is usually red. Each of the elements of the solar plexus chakra has a specific meaning.

Manipura — Solar Plexus Chakra

The Circular Shape

The circular shape of the lotus flower is common among most of the 7 chakras and represents rebirth, life, and spiritual awakening.

The Downward-Pointing Triangle

The downward-pointing triangle symbolizes the fire element that activates your personality and illuminates your path in your pursuit of success, knowledge, and wisdom.

The Fire

Fire represents the energy that propels you to move forward and show your brilliance to the world.

The Inverted Triangle

The inverted triangle symbolizes how the energy of the three lower chakras spreads up to the higher chakras.

The Ten Petals of the Lotus Flower

The ten petals of the lotus flower represent the ten *Pranas*, or energy currents and vibrations, within your body. Everyone has five *Pranas* and five *Upa Pranas*. The ten petals also represent the ten vices, stumbling blocks, or distractions that one needs to overcome to achieve knowledge, wisdom, and success. The ten vices are foolishness, shame, sadness, ambition, treachery, jealousy, disgust, delusion, fear, and ignorance in spiritual matters.

The solar plexus chakra acts as a mediator between the first two chakras, which are external, and the internal reflection of our consciousness. The root chakra focuses on the connection we have to the Earth and our ancestors; the sacral chakra focuses on the relationships we have with others and how these relationships affect us; the solar plexus chakra then shifts the focus from the external to the internal and tries to foster a better understanding of the self.

The solar plexus chakra is all about taking care of yourself, honoring yourself, and realizing the self, acting as the guiding voice in our lives. We can say that the solar plexus chakra influences the following five aspects of your life:

- **Identity:** The solar plexus chakra forms the core of your identity and personality. It allows us to discover who we truly are and allows us to show our true, authentic selves to the world.
- **Personal Power:** The third chakra also influences your personal power. It gives you the power you need to take complete control over your emotions, thoughts, and actions.
- **Willpower:** The solar plexus chakra also influences your willpower. It gives you the discipline you need to follow through your decisions and do the right thing, even when it might be difficult to do so.
- **Confidence:** This chakra also has an influence on how you view yourself and your self-esteem. A well-balanced solar plexus chakra gives you the self-assuredness you need to make your decisions.
- **Intention and Action:** Achieving knowledge, wisdom, and success is impossible without action. The third chakra gives you the power you need to take action in the life's pursuit you desire.

Whereas the root chakra and the sacral chakra are more instinctive in nature—focused on survival and pursuing pleasure—the solar plexus chakra is more conscious, as it seeks to understand who you are as a person and what you want out of life as a thinking individual. This chakra allows makes it possible for you to make conscious choices and decisions, set goals for yourself, and then take action to achieve these goals.

The solar plexus also influences our self-acceptance. A healthy solar plexus chakra makes you feel good about yourself, which affects how you allow others to treat you in business, in relationships, and so on. Someone who feels good about themselves knows their worth and will not allow others to treat them unfairly. Someone who loves themselves and feels good about themselves can also make healthy decisions and has the willpower to go after their wants unapologetically. However, someone who has poor self-acceptance also has low self-esteem and lacks the willpower to go after their wants. This makes it easy for others to manipulate and control them.

The solar plexus chakra can be considered as the seat of your personal power. Note that in this case, it is not about your power over others, but in power over yourself, which is the ability to take control over your fears, your thoughts, your emotions, and to take the right action in whatever situation you find yourself in. This is also referred to as **self-mastery**.

Some themes and behavioral and psychological functions associated with the solar plexus chakra include:

- Taking control and responsibility for your life
- Setting goals and making decisions
- Intellect and mental abilities
- Forming your own personal beliefs and opinions
- Confidence and self-assurance
- Personal identity
- Independence
- Self-discipline
- Clarity of judgments
- Expression of will
- Turning thoughts and ideas into action and reality

Signs of a Well-Balanced Solar Plexus Chakra

When you have a well-aligned solar plexus chakra, you have a clear sense of self; you are confident in yourself, and you can set the right direction for yourself, define your own goals and consciously make decisions that take you closer to these goals. In addition, someone with a well-aligned solar plexus chakra is aware of her strengths and weaknesses. She also has a realistic view of what she is capable of.

People with a well-balanced solar plexus chakra enjoy challenges and the thrill of setting their goals and then doing whatever it takes to achieve these goals. Even when they encounter setbacks and obstacles, such people will remain determined and persistent until they achieve their goals. People with a well-aligned solar plexus chakra are not afraid of failure. They understand that it is a normal part of life. Rather than feeling humiliated by failure, they take the lessons learned from the failure and then start again with the wisdom gained from their previous experience.

When you have a well-aligned solar plexus chakra, you know who you are and what you want out of life. As a result, you become more assertive in life and do not allow other people to walk on you or treat you unfairly because you are confident in yourself and know what you are worth. You are not afraid to be yourself, because the solar plexus chakra gives you the confidence to show your brilliance to the world around you.

Signs That Your Solar Plexus Chakra Is Out of Alignment

The state of your chakras is constantly changing, and try as you might to avoid it, going through situations that will cause your solar plexus chakra to go out of alignment is inevitable. There are several mindsets and habits that might cause your solar plexus chakra to be suppressed. Experiencing traumatic events can also take your solar plexus chakra out of alignment. Sometimes, traumatic events in your childhood such as bullying; strict parents or guardians; growing up with disempowering ideologies; or physical, sexual, emotional, and mental abuse can block or suppress your solar plexus chakra. In addition, criticism and rejection, even during your adulthood, can also play a huge role in getting your solar plexus chakra blocked.

So, how do you tell whether you have a blocked or misaligned solar plexus chakra? The key lies in observing your emotions, thoughts, actions, and feelings within your body. These are the channels through which an unbalanced chakra expresses itself. Some signs that could point to a blocked or unbalanced solar plexus chakra include:

Victim Mentality

If your solar plexus chakra is blocked or unbalanced, you might see yourself as a victim of circumstances. Rather than taking responsibility for your life and going after what you want, you find people, materials, and circumstances to blame for your situation in life instead. Your life expectations become low and you become pessimistic. You become shy and afraid of taking leadership positions.

Lack of Self-Confidence and Assertiveness

We have already seen that a healthy solar plexus chakra gives you the confidence to shine and show your brilliance to the world. When your solar plexus chakra is blocked, however, you lose confidence in yourself, start doubting yourself, and become afraid of showing your true self to the world. Instead of being assertive, you allow others to treat you poorly because you are afraid of speaking up for yourself.

Overcompensation

Someone with a weak or blocked solar plexus chakra will usually experience feelings of inadequacy because they are not confident in themselves. To hide these feelings, such a person might turn to overcompensation. For instance, one might start excessively glorifying themselves or showing excess bravado; however, this show of bravado is false and crumbles easily when subjected to pressure, which can even lead to depression.

Seeking Approval From Others

When you have a weak or blocked solar plexus chakra, your view of yourself and your self-identity become compromised. Rather than projecting your true self to the world and being confident in who you are, you tie your identity to the approval of others. You become a people pleaser and constantly project a false image of yourself that you hope other people will like. In addition, you don't have any personal boundaries because you feel that setting up boundaries might cause people to not like you.

Sensitivity to Criticism

This point relates closely to the previous one. Because someone with a blocked or unbalanced solar plexus chakra bases their self-identity on what others think of them, such a person is highly sensitive to criticism. For instance, if such a person is an artist and one of their pieces of work attracts lots of criticism, they might believe that they are not good at their craft and give up, rather than using the criticism to improve their craft or develop a thick skin.

Lack of Ambition or Purpose

The solar plexus chakra gives us a sense of direction, a purpose in life, and helps us discover what we want out of life while giving us the power to go after it. If you have a blocked solar plexus chakra, you will not understand what you want out of life, and you won't have any ambition or purpose. You will go through the motions, trudging through life without a clear idea where you are heading.

Physical Symptoms

A blocked solar plexus chakra can also affect your physical wellbeing. Since the solar plexus chakra influences the function of the digestive system and the organs around the stomach, many of the physical symptoms associated with an unbalanced solar plexus chakra appear around this area. Some of these symptoms include disorders of the digestive system such as ulcers, diabetes, irritable bowel syndrome (IBS), and hypoglycemia, acid reflux. You might also experience stomach upsets, constipation, and the need to pass gas frequently. In addition, you might experience sugar cravings or start putting on excessive weight around the stomach.

Other signs that could indicate a blocked or unbalanced solar plexus chakra include:

- Fear of rejection
- Low self-esteem and sense of self-importance; insecure
- Making lots of plans that never get realized; irresponsibility
- Feeling helpless and powerless, like you have no control over your life
- Lethargy and fatigue
- Bullying others or trying to be overly dominant; manipulative
- Overindulgence and overeating
- Addictive tendencies
- Dependency on others
- Lack of will and resolution
- Extreme self-demand

How to Balance the Solar Plexus Chakra

If you realize that, you have some signs and symptoms that point to a blocked or unbalanced solar plexus chakra, you will need to heal and balance this chakra if you want to regain control over your life. Question is, how do you do this? The following are some tips and strategies you can use to bring your solar plexus chakra back in alignment.

Identify the Problem

As always, the first thing you need to do when trying to heal a chakra is to identify how the misalignment of the chakra is affecting you. To do this, you need to ask yourself questions such as:

- What is your passion in life?
- Are there areas of your life where you feel passion is lacking? What are these areas?
- Which areas of your life do you feel like your power is lacking?
- Are there areas of your life you feel you have ceded your power to others?
- Are there areas where you are controlling others?
- Do you have any problems related to your digestive system?
- Are you going after your dreams?
- Do you often find yourself in codependent relationships?

Asking yourself these questions will help you identify the areas you need to focus on as you work on healing and balancing your solar plexus chakra.

Do Away With Routines, Take Risks, and Go After New Experiences

Human beings love routines—they are *safe* because you always know what to expect. Unfortunately, routines also make us get comfortable. The longer we stick to a routine, the harder it becomes for us to step out of this comfort zone. Remember, one role of the solar plexus chakra is to help us discover who we are and what we want out of life. However, it is impossible to discover anything about yourself when you are constantly going through the same safe routines. Sticking to routines can repress the solar plexus chakra.

To avoid blocking your solar plexus chakra, and to unblock it if needed, break out of your routine and start taking risks and going after new experiences. Experiment with new and different hobbies, places, cultures, and people. Experiencing something you have never experienced before will help stimulate your solar plexus chakra and get its energy flowing within your body.

Meditation

We have already established that meditation plays a critical role in bringing your chakras back into alignment. Just like the two previous chakras, meditation for the solar plexus chakra is simple. Below are the steps to follow when meditating to heal the solar plexus chakra.

- Find a comfortable, quiet place where you are unlikely to be disturbed for the duration of your meditation session. It is also advisable to wear loose-fitting, comfortable clothes. If possible, dim the lights if they are too bright.
- Sit in a position that will allow you to remain comfortable for the duration of your meditation session. Keep your back straight, push your shoulders back, and relax your limbs.
- Close your eyes and then slowly take several deep breaths, inhaling through the nose, holding the breath for a few seconds, and then exhale slowly through the mouth.
- Bring your focus to the area below your chest and between your ribs in the location of your solar plexus chakra.
- Visualize a glowing sphere of yellow light in this area, and imagine this sphere slowly becoming wider and brighter, expanding to cover your entire rib cage and the surrounding areas.

- As the sphere expands, imagine a feeling of relaxation and warmth accompanying the spreading glow. Hold this image and sensation for about five minutes.
- Slowly let go of the image of the yellow sphere of light and allow the energy to dissolve throughout your body. As the energy dissolves, slowly return your focus back to your breathing.
- After about five breaths, open your eyes slowly and allow them to adjust to the light in the room. Remain seated for a few minutes until all your focus is back in the room.

If you so wish, you can follow your meditation sessions with some affirmations which we will cover next.

Solar Plexus Chakra Affirmations

Affirmations are another great way to balance and heal an unbalanced chakra. Some affirmations you can use to heal your solar plexus chakra include:

- I am strong and courageous.
- I am confident.
- I have the power within me to do everything I desire.
- I have the power to stand up for myself.
- I have high self-esteem.
- I am whole.
- I am worthy.
- I am responsible for my life.
- I have the power to get things done easily and effortlessly.

- I am assertive and have the power to set my boundaries.

The key to making affirmations effective is to be sincere and to believe the message. The more you repeat the affirmation, the easier it becomes for your subconscious mind to believe them and reprogram your way of thinking. As the solar plexus chakra is all about confidence, it becomes even more important to repeat the affirmations as often as possible. Get into the habit of reciting these affirmations regularly, at least once every day.

Yoga for the Solar Plexus Chakra

Just like meditation, yoga is another powerful and elegant way of stimulating your body and triggering the flow of suppressed energy. Since the solar plexus chakra is in your upper abdomen, most of the yoga poses associated with realigning this chakra focus on strengthening the area around your upper abdomen and your core.

Some great yoga poses for the solar plexus chakra include:

Full Boat Pose: Also referred to as **Paripurna Navasana**, this yoga pose is great for strengthening the core. In addition, it enhances your posture, balances your entire body, stimulates your digestive system, and boosts your self-confidence. This pose should also inspire the go-getter lying within you.

Bow Pose: This yoga pose is also referred to as **Dhanurasana**. This pose is important in boosting the flow of blood and energy around the organs involved in digestion, particularly the liver. Remember, the solar plexus chakra also has influence over the function of the digestive system. The liver is important in this case because it is related to worry and anger, according to traditional Chinese medicine. Therefore, stimulating the liver through the bow pose can help eliminate worry and anger, making you more confident.

Half Boat Pose: This yoga pose is also known as **Ardha Navasana** and is a variation of the full boat pose discussed above. This pose helps strengthen the entire abdominal area and makes the energy flow in this area, stimulating the solar plexus chakra.

Spend Time Outside

Spending some time outside in the sun is a powerful way of healing a deficient or excessively blocked solar plexus chakra. The element for the solar plexus chakra is fire; therefore, the sun can act as a great source of healing vitality for this chakra. People deficient in vitamin D, which comes from the sun's energy, are more likely to struggle with anxiety and depression, so to heal your solar plexus chakra, get in the habit of spending more time outside in the sun. You can take walks, relax somewhere in your neighborhood park, or even meditate, all while out in the sun.

Avoid Critical and Negative People

We saw in the previous section that some things that contribute to a blockage of the solar plexus chakra are criticism, rejection, and negativity. Therefore, if you realize that you have relationships with people who are overly critical and negative—people who are always putting you down rather than supporting you—then you should cut these people off. Even if you are not in a position to eliminate them from your life (for instance, if such a person is part of your family), at least create some distance between you and them. Instead, spend more of your time with people who support you and encourage you to grow and go after your dreams.

Solar Plexus Chakra Healing Stones

To harmonize and heal your solar plexus chakra, you can either wear these stones as jewelry, carry them in your pocket, keep them physically near you (such as in your bedroom or office), or hold them in your hands while meditating. Some stones you can use to heal the solar plexus chakra include:

- **Tiger's Eye:** This is the most effective stone for realigning the solar plexus chakra. The semi-precious stone, which is gold with brownish stripes similar to a tiger, is great for cleansing and balancing the third chakra. It also helps **eliminate feelings of helplessness and inadequacy**.

- **Amber**: This stone is an organic gemstone that is yellowish-orange. Amber is great for cleansing and balancing the solar plexus chakra, and it is also excellent for increasing **confidence** and boosting your **mental clarity**. This stone is especially effective for those who find decision-making hard.

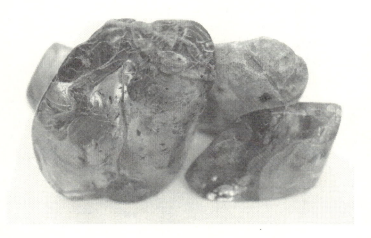

- **Yellow Tourmaline:** This is another semi-precious, yellow-colored stone with a striking appearance. Often promoted as a **detox**, it is great for ridding the body of toxic energy and negativity, especially negativity about your self-image.

Let Go of the Victim Mentality

We already saw that people with a blocked or suppressed solar plexus chakra have the tendency of seeing themselves as victims and always finding someone else to blame for their circumstances. These people believe that they are powerless to change their circumstances because they don't believe that they are responsible for the outcome of their lives. These people also forego their needs to meet the needs of others, known as **the Martyr Syndrome**. This is a very damaging mindset.

If you want to heal your solar plexus chakra, attempt to get rid of this victim mentality. To do this, start watching your thoughts and try to identify any time you think of yourself as a victim. Once you notice that you are playing victim, change the narrative and tell yourself that you are not powerless, that there is something that you can do to change the situation. Note that this will be difficult in the beginning because it requires that you step up and take responsibility for your situation when you were used to passing the responsibility to another external force. With time, however, you will get used to taking the weight of self-responsibility, and you will then be able to take control over your life again.

Change Your Diet

We have already seen that some foods are better suited to healing blocked chakras than others. Some foods that can help you unblock and balance your solar plexus chakra include whole grains which are good for digestion, such as oats, rice, rye, and spelt. Legumes such as beans, chickpeas, and lentils are also good for the solar plexus and should feature prominently in your diet. When cooking, use spices such as cinnamon, ginger, turmeric, and cumin. Make vegetables and yellow fruits part of your diet too, since they are good for digestion and balancing your solar plexus chakra. Some fruits and vegetables to add to your diet include pineapples, bananas, lemons, and yellow capsicums.

Cut Off Unhealthy Attachments

Having unhealthy attachments is a huge contributor to energy stagnation and blockage of the solar plexus chakra. When most people think of attachments, they think about attachment to other people. However, attachments can be mental, physical, or emotional. You can form an unhealthy attachment to an object, person, substance (*drugs*), fear, expectation, memory, desire, belief, or an ideal.

Attachments are energy flows that become stuck within our minds and bodies. Unfortunately, these attachments do not work towards our own good. Instead, they put limitations on our capabilities and behaviors and lead to addictions. Attachments also distort your view of the self, which contributes to a blockage of your solar plexus chakra, thus getting rid of these attachments is a crucial part to heal your solar plexus chakra.

To let go of an unhealthy attachment, ask yourself how the attachment is benefiting you. In most cases, you will realize that some attachments do not add any value to your life and are instead dragging you down. Once you realize this, you can then work on recovering and living your life without reliance on whoever or whatever it was you were excessively attached to.

Identify the Greatest Source of Resistance in Your Life

Are there some negative issues that you have to deal with constantly? Do you have some fears that seem to never go away? What issues bring the greatest anxiety in your life? Answering these questions will allow you to discover the issues that are constantly draining your energy. Often, our solar plexus chakra gets blocked or suppressed because we are fighting something in our lives. Once you discover whatever is draining your energy, you can then work on stopping the resistance and freeing up your energy.

Using the above tips and techniques in your day-to-day life will help you bring your solar plexus chakra back into alignment, which will then allow you to embrace your true, authentic self and share your brilliance with the world.

CHAPTER FIVE: THE HEART CHAKRA

The fourth chakra in the seven chakra system is the heart chakra, which is also referred to as **Anahata**. Anahata is a Sanskrit term that can translate to "unbeaten," "unstuck," or "unhurt." The heart chakra controls our ability to form deep bonds with other people, to give and receive love, and to influence our relationships with others. Therefore, the symbol of the heart is used to represent love.

The energy from the heart chakra gives us feelings of love, respect, caring, compassion, empathy, generosity, altruism, and self-love. It allows us to realize our interconnectedness to life and the universe through the relationships we have with other people. The energy from the heart chakra also gives us the ability to accept and forgive others.

Unlike the heart *organ* located towards the left part of your chest, we find the heart chakra between our breasts, at the center of our chest. Because of its location in the chest area, the heart chakra influences the function of organs within this area, including the lungs and the cardiac system. For these organs to function properly, they rely on breathing and

air, the element for the heart chakra. This chakra also influences the function of the thymus gland, which regulates the immune system and the production of hormones.

The air element of the heart chakra symbolizes the traits of love, compassion, connection, and relations. It also represents the interconnectedness of all things and spaciousness.

The heart chakra is represented by the color **green**, though some higher frequencies of the heart chakra energy have come off with a **pink** representation, which is why a pink heart usually symbolizes love. Green is another color of love; it symbolizes prosperity, abundance, and transformation. Green allows you to transform your ego and embrace love and compassion. Green also signifies life, growth, and balance. The color green is calming and soothing, and the color of nature.

The symbol of the heart chakra is a green-colored lotus flower with twelve petals. At the center of the lotus flower are two intersecting triangles, one pointing upwards and the other pointing downwards. The intersection of the two starts forms the shape of a six-pointed star.

Like with the other chakras, each of the elements of the heart chakra symbol has its own specific meaning.

The Twelve Petals of the Lotus Flower

The twelve petals of the lotus flower in the Anahata symbol represent the twelve celestial qualities that the heart represents. These twelve celestial qualities are love, unity, peace, compassion, kindness, forgiveness, harmony, bliss, purity, understanding, clarity, and empathy.

Two Intersecting Triangles

The two intersecting triangles that form the six-pointed star illustrate the intermingling of opposing energies, such as the male and female energies, or the energies of matter and spirit. The resulting star formed by the two triangles represents how these opposing energies come together harmoniously, with the heart acting as the center of the connection and integration. The six-pointed star also symbolizes the all-encompassing quality of the air element. According to some Vedic interpretations, the combination of the twelve petals and the six-pointed star show the 72,000 nadis, or energy channels, within the human body (12 x 6000 = 72,000). This also symbolizes the role of the heart chakra as the center of connection of all the subtle energy channels within the human body.

The heart chakra influences the following five aspects of your life:

- **Connection**: The energy of the heart chakra makes it possible for you to connect with other people and form deep bonds with them. This is true for both platonic and romantic relationships.
- **Unconditional Love:** The principle of unconditional love drives the heart chakra. It makes it possible for you to love yourself and others.
- **Compassion**: The ability to be compassionate comes from the heart chakra. This chakra makes it possible for you to show empathy toward others.
- **Respect**: The energy of the Anahata also makes it possible for you to show respect both to yourself and to others. It allows you to understand and respect other people's thoughts, ideas, opinions, and boundaries.

- **Forgiveness**: The heart chakra acts as the healing center. It allows you to let go of feelings of hurt from the past, to forgive those who have hurt you, and open yourself up to new experiences, despite what you might have gone through in the past.

Some meanings and psychological and behavioral characteristics associated with the heart chakra include:

- The capacity to love yourself and others
- Ability to bond and form relationships with others
- Appreciation of beauty
- Acceptance and forgiveness
- Heart-centered discernment
- Ability to grieve
- Transcending the limitations of the ego
- Connection with other people

It is good to note that the heart chakra is the *middle* chakra, between the three lower chakras and the three upper chakras. Because of this, the heart chakra acts as a point of connection and integration between the lower chakras, which focus on materialism and Earthly matters, and the upper chakras, which focus more on spirituality and higher aspirations.

Signs That Your Heart Chakra Is in Alignment

When your heart chakra is in alignment and well-balanced, you feel deeply connected to other people; you recognize and appreciate the beauty in all that is around you and you experience a harmonious exchange of energy with those around you. You find it easy to bond with and form relationships with others.

An open and well-aligned heart chakra triggers an abundance of love, compassion, and empathy. Rather than trying to shape yourself to conform to external expectations, it allows you to feel comfortable in being yourself. It also allows you to accept other people for who they are, rather than trying to get them to conform to your expectations. When your heart chakra is well-aligned, you become altruistic and have no problem showing respect to yourself and to others.

Someone with an open and balanced heart chakra is open and receptive to others. They don't struggle with feelings of bitterness, fear, isolation, or loneliness because they are not afraid of opening their hearts to others. They don't struggle with loving themselves, which allows them to show love to others. An open heart chakra also allows you to let go of the toxic behaviors and characteristics that might have defined your past relationships. You stop sacrificing your wellbeing for the sake of others and learn how to forgive both yourself and others.

Signs That Your Heart Chakra Is Out of Alignment

Like the other chakras discussed before, the heart chakra can also get out of alignment and become blocked. Blockage and unbalancing of the heart chakra can be caused by several things, such as huge changes in your environment, physical ailments, and experiences with a strong emotional charge. Negative experiences associated with love and relationships have an especially big impact on your heart chakra.

When we experience negative things in our lives, we resort

to one of two coping mechanisms – we either get defensive and shut down, or we expend more energy to fight the situation. For instance, if you just went through a breakup, you might close yourself off in an attempt to numb the pain. Someone else might react to the same situation by becoming too close to a parent or a friend, in an attempt to fight the feelings of hurt. These coping mechanisms are anchored in our heart chakra, and with time, they might cause the heart chakra to go out of alignment, either becoming blocked or excessively open.

Once your heart chakra goes out of alignment, this misalignment will manifest itself in various ways, affecting your psychological, emotional, and physical wellbeing. Some indicators that you might be dealing with a blocked or unbalanced heart chakra include:

Trouble Expressing Your Emotions

Someone who has a blocked or unbalanced heart chakra will find it hard to share and express their emotions. Instead of expressing what they are feeling, they keep their emotions bottled up. Unfortunately, this affects their ability to connect with others and takes a toll on their relationships because human relationships require sharing emotions.

Dwelling on Past Relationships

If you feel stuck and spend a lot of time dwelling on relationships that have already ended, this could be a sign that your heart chakra is blocked. A blocked heart chakra makes it impossible for you to move on and form new bonds with new people. However, since human beings have a deep-seated desire to connect and form bonds with other humans, this desire results in you pining for past relationships and wishing you could bring them back.

Holding on to Grudges

When someone hurts you, it is normal to feel anger towards the person. For most people, this anger dissipates after some time. However, if you keep grudges with people for something they did years ago, you could have a block in your heart chakra. The longer you hold on to grudges, the harder it becomes for you to experience joy and open yourself to other people.

Trust Issues

People with a well-aligned and open heart chakra are receptive to others and are comfortable opening up, which allows them to form healthy relationships. People with a blocked heart chakra, however, find it hard to trust others or open up their hearts. This can keep you from getting into meaningful relationships because you constantly bring old baggage into new relationships.

Low Self-Esteem

A well-aligned heart chakra allows you to feel comfortable in being yourself, rather than trying to conform to others' expectations of who you should be. It makes you capable of self-love. When your heart chakra is out of alignment, however, you compromise your ability to love and accept yourself, which results in feelings of low self-esteem, shyness, and being overly critical of yourself.

Pushing Others Away

If you find it hard to accept attention from others, even when you crave this attention deep down, this could be a sign that your heart chakra is blocked. This usually happens after going through a breakup. You are afraid that opening yourself to others will lead to another heartbreak; therefore, you push others away because you don't want the vulnerability that comes with opening your heart and being receptive to others.

Physical Symptoms

A blocked or unbalanced heart chakra can also affect your physical wellbeing. Since the location of the heart chakra in the chest, most physical symptoms associated with a misalignment of this chakra affect organs within the chest area. Some physical symptoms of a blocked heart chakra include:

- Bronchitis
- Breathing and cardiac problems
- Lung infections
- Illness in the diaphragm
- Hypertension
- Breast cancer

In some cases, a blocked heart chakra can even lead to suicide because the affected person might feel like they are not deserving of love and *Prana* (the universal life force).

Other Psychological Symptoms

Besides the behaviors discussed above, a blocked or misaligned heart chakra can also lead to a slew of other psychological signs and symptoms, such as:

- Inability to forgive others
- Envy and jealousy
- Abusive and yearning for absolute control in relationships; lacking empathy
- Avoiding social interactions
- Withdrawal; social anxiety
- Codependence on others; lack of personal boundaries; people pleaser
- Martyr syndrome
- Victim mentality
- Fear of intimacy
- Sense of dread and heaviness in the chest area

How to Heal and Activate Your Heart Chakra

Healing and activating the heart chakra is all about cleansing, clearing blockages, strengthening, and bringing the heart chakra back into alignment. Below are some tips and techniques you can use to heal and activate your heart chakra.

Identify the Problem

Healing and activating the heart chakra is all about cleansing, clearing blockages, strengthening, and bringing the heart chakra back into alignment. Below are some tips and techniques you can use to heal and activate your heart chakra. As always, the first step of healing any unaligned chakra is to identify how its misalignment affects you. To do this, ask yourself the following questions:

- Are there areas in your life where you feel out of love?
- Are there things you truly hate? If yes, why do you hate them?
- Do you have a problem expressing love? Are you expressing love enough?
- Are there things you love but are not doing? Why are you not doing them?
- Are you kind to others? Are there ways you can improve on this?
- Do you have trouble bonding with other people?
- Do you have trouble trusting other people?
- Do you hold on to grudges?
- Do you dwell on past relationships?
- Do you have trouble forgiving others?

Answering these questions will help you realize the areas of your life affected by a blockage of the heart chakra, and you can then focus on improving these areas.

Heart Chakra Meditation

Incorporating chakra meditation into your daily routine is a powerful and effective way of healing a blocked or unbalanced chakra. Below is a simple heart chakra meditation technique you can practice every day to bring your heart chakra back into alignment.

- Find a comfortable, quiet place where you are unlikely to be disturbed for the duration of your meditation session. It is also advisable to wear loose-fitting, comfortable clothes. If possible, dim the lights if they are too bright.
- Sit in a position that will allow you to remain comfortable for the duration of your meditation session. Keep your back straight, push your shoulders back, and relax your limbs.
- Close your eyes and then slowly take several deep breaths, inhaling through the nose, holding the breath for a few seconds, then exhale slowly through the mouth.
- Picture yourself drawing energy from the base of your spine and upwards towards where the location of your heart chakra.
- Visualize the energy you just drew coming together to form a brightly glowing ball of green light at the center of your chest. Imagine this glowing ball of green light slowly expanding to cover your entire chest and ribcage. As the ball grows larger, imagine a feeling of warmth and relaxation enveloping every area the ball of light touches.
- Imagine that the ball of light represents feelings of love for yourself and others. As the ball of light continues expanding, imagine that these are feelings of love radiating from your heart chakra throughout your whole body. Hold this image and sensation for about five minutes.
- Slowly let go of the image of the yellow sphere of light and allow the energy to dissolve throughout your body. As the energy dissolves, slowly return your focus back to your breathing.
- After about five breaths, open your eyes slowly and

allow them to adjust to the light in the room. Remain seated for a few minutes until all your focus is back in the room.

You can follow this meditation session with heart chakra affirmations, which we will cover next.

Use Heart Chakra Affirmations

We have already seen that affirmations are also an effective way of healing a blocked or unbalanced chakra, especially when you couple them with meditation and chakra healing stones. Below are some affirmations you can use to heal your heart chakra.

- My heart is open to love.
- I choose love, compassion, and joy.
- I don't carry any wounds from the past.
- I am loved and wanted.
- I forgive myself and others.
- I live in a state of love, compassion, and gratefulness.
- I create loving, meaningful relationships that are good for me.
- I am in control of my own emotions.
- I love the beauty of the world and nature.
- Love resides in my heart.

Heart-Opening Yoga Poses

When our heart chakra is closed off, it means we are incapable of loving others or being loved. Fortunately, we can use heart-opening yoga poses to open up a closed-off heart chakra. When you practice these yoga poses, your heart becomes exposed, allowing the flow of energy through your heart chakra. Some heart-opening yoga poses great for healing your heart chakra include:

Cobra Pose: Also referred to as **Bhujangasana**, this yoga pose helps expand the chest area, revitalizes the circulatory system and enhances spinal strength, and is an effective pose for opening the heart chakra.

Eagle Pose: This yoga pose is also known as **Garudasana**. Not only does this pose improve your balance and strength, but it is also great at opening up the heart chakra.

Cat Pose: Also referred to as **Marjaryasana**, this pose helps eliminate tension in the back and spine. This tension contributes to a closed-off heart chakra.

Add Green Into Your Life

Since green is the color of the heart chakra, adding more green into your life can also help to heal and activate the heart chakra. You can add more green into your life by wearing green clothing, decorating your living and working spaces with green accents, eating more greens, spending time with nature, adding green plants into your living and working spaces, or painting your nails green.

Heart Chakra Stones

Wearing, holding, and meditating with chakra stones it a good way to balance and realign a blocked or unbalanced chakra and getting your energy flowing. Some stones efficient for balancing the heart chakra include:

- **Jade**: This gemstone is usually green. We associate jade with **emotional healing**, and it is especially effective when you are trying to cope with emotional injury or loss.

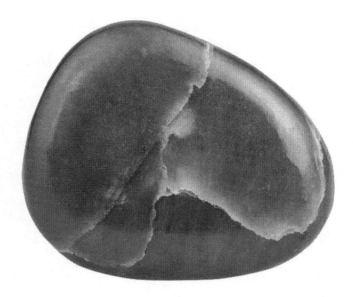

- **Green Calcite:** We consider this stone a **detoxifying** stone that helps eliminate negativity. It is great for those who are trying to feel more empathetic.

- **Green Aventurine**: This stone is believed to be effective in soothing difficult emotions. We associate it with **inspiration, vitality**, and **energy**.

Changing Your Diet

You can bring your heart chakra back into alignment by changing your diet and eating foods that stimulate its energy center. Some foods great for the heart chakra include green foods such as green bell peppers, kale, spinach, limes, and green apples, and foods rich in vitamin C. Fruits such as strawberries, oranges, and guavas will also work wonders. In addition, rich and warm soups can also help to reinvigorate your heart chakra.

Show Gratitude and Kindness

One of the most effective ways of healing your heart chakra is to show gratitude. Sitting down and thinking about all the things you are thankful for can do amazing things for your heart chakra. You can start a gratitude journaling, in which you write everything you are grateful for each day before you sleep.

Besides showing gratitude, performing random acts of kindness for other people can also help strengthen your heart chakra. However, when doing this, do not do it because you feel it is an obligation you have to perform to heal your heart chakra. Instead, do it from a point of sincerity; otherwise, you will not be healing your heart chakra.

Be Empathetic

In today's hurried and busy world, it is easy to judge others and make rash conclusions about them. This is something that makes it hard for us to connect with these people from a neutral position and ends up blocking our heart chakra. If you want to bring your heart chakra back into alignment, get into the habit of practicing empathy. Instead of judging someone, try to understand what they are going through and what it is like to be them. This will allow you to relate with others from a more loving point of view.

CHAPTER SIX: THE THROAT CHAKRA

The fifth chakra in the chakra ladder is the throat chakra. This chakra is also the first of the upper chakras, which are spiritual in nature. We can also refer to the throat chakra as **Vishuddha**, which is a Sanskrit term comprising two words: *visha,* which means "poison" or "impurity," and *suddhi,* which means "to purify." The term *vishuddha* in its entirety means "purification."

The throat chakra is all about communication and the ability to express yourself—expressing your creativity, your purpose in life, and your truth. The energy of the throat chakra pushes us to express our authentic voice without the limitations placed on us by family and cultural conditioning. The energy of this chakra also seeks to eliminate negative thinking and doubt from our lives. The throat chakra links closely to the sacral chakra, which influences our creativity and emotions.

The throat chakra influences the following five aspects of our lives:

- **Expression:** The throat chakra influences our creativity and gives us the ability to express and share this creativity with the world.
- **Truth:** The energy from the throat chakra motivates us to seek the truth with persistence and also gives us the courage to share our truth with others.
- **Integrity:** The throat chakra motivates us to uphold our integrity, stand up for what we believe in, and always be honest with ourselves.
- **Originality:** The energy of the throat chakra inspires us to be creative and to come up with original ideas that express our authentic self.
- **Communication:** The energy of the throat chakra also makes it possible for us to communicate our thoughts, ideas, and opinions effectively to others. It also gives us the ability to be good listeners.

As the name implies, the location of the throat chakra is in your neck, in the area around the throat. Its exact location is between the third and the fifth vertebrae. The throat chakra allows energy to pass between the head and the lower parts of the body. It's good to note that the throat chakra is a multi-dimensional chakra; it starts from the front of the throat and through the back, rising slightly as it exits out of the back of the neck.

Like the other chakras, the throat chakra affects the function of the organs surrounding it. The throat chakra associates with the mouth, teeth, palate, tongue, jaws, esophagus, pharynx, the pharyngeal and branchial plexi, trachea, nose, ears, neck, carotid arteries, and the shoulders. It also influences the function of the thyroid, which is the gland that regulates metabolism, growth, and body temperature. It also influences the function of the endocrine system, which is responsible for the production of hormones.

The element used to represent the throat chakra is **ether**, which symbolizes purification, authenticity, and communication. Ether also represents the spaciousness around the neck and throat area, which allows the flow of insightful spiritual truths.

Blue is the represented color of the throat chakra, along with various shades such as aquamarine and turquoise. Sometimes, a smoky purple or turquoise shade may represent the energy of the throat chakra. The color blue is used because it symbolizes truth, wisdom, trust, faith, and loyalty. Blue also symbolizes the clarity of communication associated with the throat chakra, which compares to the bright blue color of clear skies.

The symbol for the throat chakra is a bluish lotus flower with sixteen petals. At the center of the lotus flower is a downward-pointing triangle with another circle inscribed inside it. Every element of the throat chakra has a specific meaning.

The Lotus Flower with Sixteen Petals

The lotus flower with sixteen petals symbolizes the sixteen vowels of the Sanskrit language. These vowels are light and pronouncing them is easy. Therefore, using the sixteen petals illustrates the airy quality of communication. In addition, the number sixteen transforms to the number seven in numerology by adding one to six to come up with a single digit. In numerology, the number seven associates with awareness, understanding, and knowledge.

The Inverted Triangle

The inverted triangle inside the lotus flower symbolizes the upward movement of energy and the transformation of knowledge into enlightenment. The triangle also symbolizes the expression of our higher consciousness.

The Circle

The circle inscribed inside the inverted triangle symbolizes the full moon, which is a representation of a purified mind. Remember, *vishuddha* stands for purification.

Besides influencing communication and expression, the throat chakra also helps you connect to your spirit. It acts as a link between the heart chakra and the upper chakras of the head, allowing the flow of energy between these chakras and allowing you to access your higher self.

Signs of a Well-Aligned Throat Chakra

When your throat chakra is well-aligned, you feel confident in yourself and can communicate effectively. Someone with a well-aligned throat chakra is also more sensitive to the energies of those around them, and they feel more at ease in the world. In addition, a well-aligned throat chakra might cause more vivid dreams and a high ability to recall those dreams. A well-aligned throat chakra will also enhance your creativity.

We strengthen our ability to listen to and follow the guidance of our inner voice when we balance our throat chakra. When the energy of the throat chakra flows freely, there is a seamless connection between your inner world and the outer world, to where you don't feel like they are two different worlds. This makes you feel comfortable expressing your inner truth because both your inner and outer worlds seem to have merged.

It's good to note that just because the throat chakra influences our ability to communicate and express ourselves, this does not mean that someone with a well-aligned throat chakra speaks out whatever comes to their mind without thinking. Instead, the energy of the throat chakra makes you an effective communicator who knows what to say, when to say it and how to say it, while putting the feelings of others into consideration. A well-aligned throat chakra gives you perfect mastery over the communication process. You know how to select your words with mastery and pair them with the right gestures and expressions to convey your message.

Signs That Your Throat Chakra Is Out of Alignment

Sometimes, your throat chakra might get blocked or out of alignment, causing the flow of energy either to become suppressed or go into overdrive. This blockage or misalignment of the throat chakra manifests itself through various psychological, emotional, and physical symptoms.

Since the throat chakra influences communication and self-expression, blockage of this chakra impacts your ability to communicate effectively. You become unable to speak freely because you are afraid that others will judge or ridicule you. It becomes difficult for you to share your truth with the world. A blocked throat chakra also affects your ability to express yourself confidently. You become introverted, insecure, and timid. You avoid expressing your wants and desires because you don't have confidence in yourself.

Because of the lack of confidence, insecurity, and timidity, you might start feeling uncomfortable around people, and as a result, you avoid social situations entirely. This lack of confidence also makes you distrust your inner voice. If your throat chakra is excessively open, your behavior will be on the other end of the spectrum. You become mean, verbally aggressive, and have the urge to talk or gossip endlessly. The filter that normally separates what you are thinking and what comes out of your mouth becomes dysfunctional.

Other symptoms of a blocked or misaligned throat chakra include shyness, fear of speaking, speech impediments, reduced creativity, stubbornness, social anxiety, arrogance, deceptiveness, being manipulative, inability to listen to others or keep your word, lying, and failure to keep secrets.

Besides the above psychological symptoms, you might also experience physical symptoms such as sore throat, hoarseness, headaches, neck pain, mouth ulcers, dental issues, disorders of the jaw, laryngitis, thyroid problems, colds, and hearing problems.

How To Heal And Activate The Throat Chakra

If you are experiencing any of the above symptoms because of a blocked or unbalanced throat chakra, you need to heal and activate the throat chakra to get rid of the problems. Below are some tips and techniques you can use to heal and activate a blocked throat chakra.

Identify The Problem

The first step to healing your throat chakra is to identify how the blockage is affecting you. To do this, you need to ask yourself the following questions:

- Are there times when I'm not speaking my truth?
- Are there areas where I'm not expressing myself fully?
- Are there things I need to say that I'm not?
- Are there some things I'm talking about too much?
- Are there times when I feel I don't have the freedom to express myself? Why?
- Do I feel like there is a disparity between my inner and outer worlds?

Answering these questions will allow you to identify how your throat chakra is affecting you, which will show you what areas you need to focus on when healing your throat chakra.

Throat Chakra Meditation

Meditating a few times per week can be very effective in healing your throat chakra. In addition, most meditation techniques are fairly easy, even for someone who has never meditated before. Below is a simple meditation technique you can use to heal your throat chakra:

- Find a quiet place and sit down somewhere you will be comfortable.
- Close your eyes and take ten deep breaths, breathing in through your nose and breathing out through the mouth.
- Progressively relax all the muscles in your body, starting with the head and moving down to your toes.
- After you relax your body, visualize a glowing ball of blue light spinning around your throat area.

- Imagine the ball of light growing bigger and expanding outwards all over your body. As the ball expands, imagine it dissolving all the obstructions inhibiting the flow of energy within you.
- Hold this feeling for about five minutes, and then slowly return your focus back to your breathing.
- After about five breaths, open your eyes slowly and allow them to adjust to the light in the room. Remain seated for a few minutes until all your focus is back in the room.

With that, your throat chakra meditation technique is now complete.

Throat Chakra Affirmations

Repeating throat chakra affirmations every day is another powerful way of healing your throat chakra. Below are some effective throat chakra affirmations you can use:

- I am entitled to speak my truth.
- I am honest and clear in my communication.
- I am at peace with myself.
- I love sharing my wisdom and experiences.
- I express my feelings with ease.
- I know what my truth is.
- I know how to listen to others.
- I am a person of integrity.

Throat Chakra Yoga Poses

You can use yoga poses that focus on simple head and neck

movements to unblock a blocked throat chakra. Some effective yoga poses for healing the throat chakra include:

Fish Pose: Also referred to as **Matsyasana**, this yoga pose stimulates and balances the throat chakra by strengthening and stretching the neck muscles.

King Pigeon Pose: This yoga pose is also referred to as **Kapotasana**. This pose stretches the throat and entire front body, thus allowing the flow of energy through your throat chakra.

Upward Plank: Also referred to as **Purvottanasana**, this pose eliminates blockages in the throat chakra by stretching your shoulders and upper arms.

Throat Chakra Healing Stones

You can also heal your throat chakra by carrying, wearing, holding, or being in the close vicinity of throat chakra healing stones. You can also use the stones during meditation. Some powerful throat chakra healing stones include:

Lapis Lazuli: Also referred to as the "stone of truth," this semi-precious stone is great for those who are trying to become more **honest** in their communication.

Aquamarine: Associated with **acceptance** and **courage**, this stone is great for those who want to become more effective communicators, especially in close relationships.

Turquoise: This semi-precious stone is quite effective for those who want to become more **confident** in their communication.

Add Blue to Your Life

Since the color blue represents the throat chakra, adding this color into your life can also help you heal and realign it. To add more blue into your life, you can wear blue colored clothes, wear blue colored jewelry, use more blue to decorate your house, paint your nails blue, and so on. Meditating on the color blue is also an effective way of healing your fifth chakra.

Get a Neck Massage

Getting a neck massage can also help break up any blockages within your neck muscles and redistribute any stuck energy in this area. If you use this technique, get the neck massage from a professional masseur.

Express Your Feelings

Talking openly about your feelings with your family and friends is great for healing and balancing your throat chakra. As you talk about these feelings, this stimulates the flow of energy within your throat chakra. If you find it hard to verbalize your feelings, you can still express them by writing them down in your personal journal. Get in the habit of writing your thoughts and feelings every night before you go to bed.

CHAPTER SEVEN: THE THIRD EYE CHAKRA

The third eye chakra is the second-highest chakra. It is the center of our foresight and intuition, driven by the principles of imagination and openness. The Sanskrit term for the third eye chakra is **Ajna**, which translates to "perceive" or "command." This is a reference to the wisdom and higher understanding that we gain through a balancing of the third eye chakra. According to yogic metaphysics, the third eye chakra allows us to access a kind of perception created by the mind and not based on reality. A well-aligned third eye chakra allows us to move towards spiritual enlightenment and develop an intuitive sensibility.

In addition, the third eye chakra makes it possible for us to trust the inner voice that guides us in life; it gives us direction and allows us to use our natural talents to achieve the life we dream of. A well-balanced third eye chakra brings together the functions of the other five chakras.

Many people assume that they would locate the third eye chakra at the center of the forehead, which is wrong. The location of the third eye chakra is above the bridge of your nose, just between your eyebrows. Sometimes, the third eye chakra is also said to be inside the head, just behind the eyes.

Unlike the other chakras discussed previously that associate with the body's organs and glands, the third eye chakra only relates to one gland: the pineal gland, which is in our brain close to the optic nerves. The pineal gland has to do with the perception of changes in lighting and visual stimulations and regulates biorhythms, including waking and sleep time.

Another difference between the third eye chakra and the other lower chakras is that unlike the other chakras, there is **no element** correlated to the third eye chakra. We can attribute this to how the third eye chakra is beyond physicality.

The third eye chakra influences the following five aspects of our lives:

- **Wisdom**: The sixth chakra acts as the seat of our knowledge and wisdom and makes it possible for our minds to achieve a profound understanding.
- **Intuition**: The energy of the third eye chakra allows us to develop intuitive sensibility and gives us an inner perception for perceiving subtle aspects of reality.
- **Self-reflection**: This chakra makes it possible for you to self-reflect and examine your life.
- **Vision**: Like your physical eyes, the third eye chakra acts as a link between the outside world and your mind. It allows you to perceive the outer world in subtle ways.
- **Logic and creativity:** This chakra also gives you the ability to think logically and allows you to unlock your creativity.

The color **purple** or a bluish shade of purple is used to represent the third eye chakra. Sometimes a bluish-white or transparent purple represents the energy of this chakra. Purple represents the soft radiance and luminescence of the third eye chakra.

The symbol for the third eye chakra is composed of a two-petalled lotus flower with an inverted triangle inside it.

The Lotus Flower with Two Petals

The inverted triangle and the lotus flower are both linked to wisdom. In addition, the lotus flower with two petals represents the duality between God and the self.

The Inverted Triangle

The inverted triangle symbolizes the gathering and expansion of the energies and knowledge of the lower chakras into divine consciousness and the achievement of true enlightenment. This symbolism couples with the wisdom of both the inverted triangle and the lotus flower.

Some of the other traits and characteristics associated with the third eye chakra include:

- Inspiration and creativity
- Psychic abilities
- Connection to insight and wisdom
- Vision, intuition, and ability to develop accurate gut feelings
- Illumination and access to mystical states
- Perception of higher dimensions

Signs of a Well-Aligned Third Eye Chakra

When you have an open and well-aligned third eye chakra, you will have the ability to think logically and use your feelings when making big life decisions. Someone who has a balanced third eye chakra also knows of their purpose in life and works towards achieving this purpose. You become more creative and develop the ability to trust in your intuition and gut feelings. In addition, a balanced third eye chakra unlocks unprecedented levels of wisdom and moves you closer to spiritual enlightenment.

Signs of an Unbalanced Third Eye Chakra

There are several things and experiences that might contribute to a block or unbalanced third eye chakra. These include being brought up in a closed-minded family in which children were to obey without question and where guardians discourage freethinking; growing up in a family where there was no emotional stability; being ignored; having your passion or vocation belittled; losing your job; going through a life-threatening illness; experiencing significant changes in your life; and going through a divorce or bereavement.

Some signs that your third eye chakra might be unbalanced or blocked include:

- **Feeling Lost in Life:** When your third eye chakra is blocked, you have no sense of purpose in life; you feel lost, and might become dogmatic as you try to find things that can give meaning to your life.
- **A Negative Imagination:** Someone with a blocked or unbalanced throat chakra may be highly imaginative, but their imagination is negative, leading to feelings such as worry about the future and regrets about the past.
- **Trying to Figure Everything Out:** Besides worry and regret, you feel the need to have everything figured out and are very uncomfortable with uncertainty. This makes you unable to enjoy the present and can even lead to insomnia.
- **Endless Frustration**: Someone with an unbalanced third eye chakra becomes attached to the need for

things to turn out as they want. As life is full of surprises, they also experience endless frustration for when life does not go their way.
- **Physical Symptoms:** An unbalanced or blocked third eye chakra can lead to physical symptoms such as front/upper sinus conditions, disorders of the brain, ear and eye disorders, frequent headaches, dementia, mental illnesses, brain tumors, and neurological disorders.
- **Other Symptoms:** Other symptoms of a blocked or unbalanced third eye chakra include indecisiveness, lack of trust in your purpose, paranoia, feeling pointless and insignificant in life, lack of ethics, anxiety and depression, and problems with learning.

How to Heal and Activate the Third Eye Chakra

If you are experiencing any of the above symptoms that are linked with a blocked or unbalanced third eye chakra, the following are some techniques you can use to heal and activate this chakra.

Identify the Problem

As always, the first step to healing and realigning a blocked or unbalanced chakra is to identify ways in which the chakra might be affecting you. To do this, you need to introspect and ask yourself questions such as:

- Do I have thoughts I wish I didn't have? Why am I thinking about these thoughts?

- Are there situations where I do not have the whole picture but still feel that I need to address something?
- Are there aspects of my life that I am not willing to look at? Why?
- Do I constantly think about the negative aspects of life?
- Do I know my purpose in life?

Once you can figure out how the misalignment of your third eye chakra is affecting you, you can then focus on making improvements in these areas.

Third Eye Chakra Meditation

Just like with the other five chakras, meditation is great for healing an unbalanced third eye chakra. Below is a simple meditation technique you can use to heal your third eye chakra, even if you have no prior experience with meditation.

- Find a comfortable, quiet place where you are unlikely to be disturbed for the duration of your meditation session.
- Sit in a position that will allow you to remain comfortable for the duration of your meditation session.
- Close your eyes and then slowly take several deep breaths, inhaling through the nose, holding the breath for a few seconds, then exhale slowly through the mouth.
- Focus your attention on the location of the third eye chakra, which is the area between your eyebrows.

Visualize a purple-colored ball of light glowing in this area.
- Imagine this ball of light expanding and becoming increasingly warmer. Feel its energy washing all over your body. Hold this image and sensation for about five minutes.
- Slowly let go of the image of the purple ball of light and allow the energy to dissolve throughout your body. As the energy dissolves, slowly return your focus back to your breathing.
- After about five breaths, open your eyes slowly and allow them to adjust to the light in the room. Remain seated for a few minutes until all your focus is back in the room.

That concludes your third eye chakra meditation technique. It is good to note that consistent meditation is one of the most crucial factors if you want to keep your third eye chakra aligned. Meditation helps you maintain a heightened state of consciousness after you have activated your third eye chakra.

Third Eye Chakra Yoga Poses

Just like with the other five chakras, yoga poses are great for unblocking a blocked third eye chakra. Some great yoga poses for unblocking this chakra include:

Child's Pose: This pose, also known as **Balasana**, focuses your attention inwards and stimulates the flow of the energy of the third eye chakra.

Hero Pose: This seated yoga pose, known as **Virasana**, is great for cleansing and healing the third eye chakra because it is the perfect yoga pose for meditation—one of the best ways of activating the third eye chakra.

Big Toe: This yoga pose, also referred to as **Padangusthasana**, is another effective pose for stimulating the energy of the third eye chakra.

Third Eye Chakra Affirmations

Infusing your mind with positive affirmations can also help to activate and balance your third eye chakra. Some affirmations you could use to activate this chakra include:

- I trust in myself.
- I trust and follow the guidance of my inner voice.
- I am on my true path.
- I trust in my intuition.
- My third eye is open.
- I am an intuitive person who knows what is right for me.
- I have unlimited possibilities.
- I am aware of my purpose in life.

Explore Different Perspectives

We already saw that being closed-minded can contribute to having a blocked third eye chakra. Therefore, to keep yours open, try to find new perspectives and viewpoints by interacting with people from diverse backgrounds, watching different programs, reading books, and trying new things.

Third Eye Chakra Healing Stones

Find some precious stones associated with the third eye chakra and use them to heal this chakra by either wearing them as jewelry, using them to meditate, carrying them in your pocket or bag, or holding them in your hand even when having a relaxing evening. Some effective stones for healing the third eye chakra include:

- **Purple Fluorite:** This gemstone is useful for those who are trying to sharpen their **intuition** and improve their **decision-making** abilities.

- **Amethyst**: This is a beautiful gemstone that is associated with **wisdom**, and is great for someone who is trying to relieve headaches related to the third eye chakra.

- **Black Obsidian:** This stone is also great for healing the third eye chakra and is believed to bring **balance** between **reason** and **emotion**.

Change Your Limiting Beliefs

Like closed-minded, having limiting beliefs can also contribute to the blockage and unbalancing of the third eye chakra. In most cases, these beliefs fill you with self-doubt and make you lose confidence in yourself. To activate and stimulate your third eye chakra, you need to identify any such beliefs you might have and work on changing these beliefs.

Observe Your Thoughts

One contributor to a blocked or unbalanced third eye chakra is that we often believe our thoughts are our identity; however, our thoughts are not who we are. Our thoughts are random, and they don't define who we are. Once you learn to observe your thoughts and understand that they are temporary and do not define who you are, you will be on your way to self-mastery, which will activate and stimulate your third eye chakra.

Other Techniques

Aside from the techniques discussed above, other techniques you can use to heal the third eye chakra include listening to sounds in the 852 Hz frequency, fostering creativity in yourself, getting in touch with your feelings, lucid dreaming and divinations, and being more mindful.

CHAPTER EIGHT: THE CROWN CHAKRA

The crown chakra is the topmost chakra in the chakra ladder. Being the topmost chakra, the crown chakra grants us access to higher states of consciousness and spiritual wisdom. This chakra acts as the gate pass to the universe, allowing us to tap into the universal energy. The crown chakra also connects by energy to the root chakra, as they are both at the extreme ends of the seven chakra system. The energy of this chakra helps us to transcend all our personal limitations. We can refer to the crown chakra as **Sahasrara** in Sanskrit, which translates to "thousand petals."

The location of the crown chakra is at the top center of the head or hovering slightly above the head. Just like a crown, it sits atop of the head radiating its energy upwards. The main organs associated with the crown chakra are the pituitary gland, pineal gland, and the hypothalamus. The role of the pituitary gland and the hypothalamus is to regulate the production of hormones within the body. The pineal gland, as we have seen, regulates our waking and sleeping time and is sensitive to changes in light. Besides these glands, the crown chakra also influences the function of the brain, eyes, ears, nervous system, muscular system, skeletal system, and skin.

Just like the third eye chakra, the crown chakra does not associate with any element because it is beyond physicality. The crown chakra is represented by the color **violet**, though sometimes white is used. On occasion, the color gold is also used to represent the energy of the crown chakra.

Violet represents the crown chakra because it is a very spiritual color; it has the strongest vibration and shortest wavelength of all the colors that make up the visible spectrum, and it symbolizes an inner sense of wholeness and oneness. It also symbolizes rebirth, the end of a cycle, and the rise of something new. Violet also signifies illumination, peace and tranquility of reflective change, and the happiness of transformation. It also symbolizes access to higher realms beyond our material and physical reality. Therefore, this color can represent mystery, magic, mysticism, rituals, cleansing, and purification.

The crown chakra's symbol is of a violet lotus flower with a thousand petals.

The Thousand Petals

These petals, which sometimes show as white, are the ones referenced in the term Sahasrara. The thousand petals on the lotus flower symbolizes the unity we have with the universe and other beings, and the connection of this chakra to the divine. The petals also represent prosperity, purity, renewal, and beauty.

The Circle

The circle of the lotus flower associates with the full moon, which symbolizes the awakening of the mind into consciousness.

The crown chakra affects the following five aspects of your life:

- **Recognizing Beauty**: The energy of the crown chakra makes it possible for you to recognize divinity and beauty in all things.
- **Unity**: The highest chakra also unites you with the

universe. It is a point of connection between you and those around you and the universe in its entirety.
- **Awareness**: The crown chakra allows us to access higher consciousness and achieve transcendental awareness.
- **Enlightenment**: By acting as a connection between the mind and higher states of consciousness, the crown chakra allows you to achieve the utmost clarity and spiritual wisdom.
- **Serenity and Bliss:** A well-aligned crown chakra brings with it feelings of deep peace, joy, and serenity.

Signs of a Well-Aligned Crown Chakra

Yogic philosophy states that the Sahasrara is the seat of our soul and allows us to achieve spiritual enlightenment. While not everyone who has a well-aligned crown chakra will achieve this spiritual enlightenment, the alignment of this chakra will allow you to achieve profound levels of clarity and inner peace. In addition, it will fill you with a sense of interconnectedness and belonging to the people around you and the universe. You will no longer experience any sense of isolation.

Rather than feeling tired with life, aligning the crown chakra will make you feel rejuvenated, and you will start seeing the beauty in everything around you. If you previously had problems with a rigid identity and were excessively egotistical, you can let go of this burden and feel more playful and light. A balanced crown chakra will also allow you to live in the present and to see the bigger picture of your life. In addition, a great sense of serenity and expansiveness will overcome your life.

Signs of an Unbalanced Crown Chakra

Just like the other six chakras below it, the crown chakra can also become blocked or get out of alignment. Some things that might unbalance your crown chakra include:

- Fear, stress, and anxiety
- Sickness
- Involved in an accident; experiencing losses
- Fear of change
- Ego and conflicts
- Emotional upsets; repressed emotions
- Shallow relationships
- Poor sleep quality
- Information overload; not trusting information received

In addition, if the third eye chakra is unbalanced, it can also cause an imbalance in the crown chakra as it (the crown chakra) overcompensates for the imbalance in the third eye chakra.

Once the crown chakra becomes unbalanced, the flow of energy through the chakra becomes disrupted. This disruption causes disharmony within the body, resulting in a variety of mental, emotional, and physical symptoms within the body.

- Some emotional and psychological symptoms of a blocked crown chakra include:

- Lack of direction; inability to set goals or work towards achieving them
- Inability to connect with others; loneliness and isolation
- Feelings of spiritual disconnection; not knowing your spiritual path
- Inactive or dysfunctional intuition; weird dreams
- Lack of clarity
- Fear, anxiety, depression,
- Boredom and frustration,
- Mental illness; learning difficulties,
- Sense of elitism; greed and materialism

Aside from the emotional and psychological symptoms, one might also experience physical symptoms that go along with them, such as frequent headaches, insomnia and other sleeping problems, nerve pain and neurological disorders, schizophrenia and other delusional disorders, Alzheimer's, disorders of the thyroid and pineal gland, comas, chronic fatigue, sensitivity to light, sinus pain, dizziness, sore eyes, paralysis, dementia, epilepsy, senility, multiple sclerosis, Parkinson's disease, and disorders of the endocrine system.

How to Heal and Activate Your Crown Chakra

If you have any of the above symptoms related to a blocked or unbalanced crown chakra, you need to heal the chakra, not only as a way of getting rid of these problems but also so you can achieve a sense of serenity, bliss, and enlightenment. Below are some techniques you can use to heal and activate your crown chakra.

Identify the Problem

So far, you already know that the first thing you need to do when trying to heal or activate a blocked or unbalanced chakra is to identify how the blockage or misalignment is affecting you. For the crown chakra, some questions you need to ask yourself to identify the problem include:

- Do I feel connected to my soul? Is there something I can do to make myself feel connected? What is keeping me from doing it?
- What are my beliefs about life and death? How did I form these beliefs?
- Am I ready to let go of my life when the time comes?
- Are there things that I have not accomplished in life that I could let go? What is keeping me from doing these things?

As you answer these questions, you will start noticing the areas of your life that are being affected by the blocked or unbalanced crown chakra, and you can then pay greater attention to these areas while healing your crown chakra.

Crown Chakra Meditation

Meditation is the most powerful and the most effective way of healing and activating the crown chakra, owing to the strong link between this chakra and spirituality. Fortunately, meditation techniques for the crown chakra are as simple as those for the other chakras. Below is an easy meditation technique you can use to heal your crown chakra:

- Find a comfortable, quiet place where you are

unlikely to be disturbed for the duration of your meditation session.
- Sit in a comfortable position, with your feet on the flow and with your back straight.
- Place your hands on your laps with your palms turned upwards in the *mudra* position. This position allows you to receive the universe's energy.
- Close your eyes and then slowly take several deep breaths, inhaling through the nose, holding the breath for a few seconds, and then exhale slowly through the mouth.
- Visualize a lotus flower sitting atop your head. Imagine its petals opening slowly, releasing a bright white or violet light.
- Picture this light becoming brighter and warmer and then pouring off the top of your head and covering your whole body. Imagine this light clearing blockages everywhere it touches. Hold this image and sensation for about five minutes.
- Slowly let go of the image of the white or violet light and slowly return your focus back to your breathing.
- After about five breaths, open your eyes slowly and allow them to adjust to the light in the room. Remain seated for a few minutes until all your focus is back in the room.

Your crown chakra meditation technique is now complete.

Crown Chakra Yoga Poses

Like the other chakras, you can also realign the crown chakra by using yoga poses. Some great yoga poses you can use to heal the crown chakra include:

Plow: We also refer to this inverted yoga pose as **Halasana**. It stretches and strengthens your shoulders and spine and is great for balancing and soothing the crown chakra.

Lotus Pose: This is a seated pose also called as **Padmasana**. It stimulates your core and spine while at the same time calming your topmost chakra.

Supported Headstand: While it is a bit advanced, this yoga pose, also referred to as Salamba **Sirsasana**, is great for crown chakra healing and balancing because it supplies blood and oxygen to your head.

Use Crown Chakra Healing Stones

You already know so far that healing stones are a simple yet effective way of healing a blocked chakra. Some of the stones you can use for healing the crown chakra include:

- **Selenite**: This somewhat clear-colored stone is very effective for realigning the crown chakra. It **eliminates stagnation**, pushes you forward in life, and opens your **awareness** to higher planes.

- **Clear Quartz:** This is another clear-colored stone. It helps amplify your **psychic** abilities, improves your **memory**, enhances your **consciousness**, gives you a heightened **awareness**, stimulates the nervous system, and encourages **clarity**, all of which is good for your crown chakra.

- **Diamond**: Like the other two stones, diamonds are also clear-colored. Diamond is great for **clearing energy fields** and facilitating your **connection** to higher planes.

Crown Chakra Affirmations

We have already established that using positive affirmations can help you reprogram your mind and heal a blocked chakra. Some affirmations you can use to heal your crown chakra include:

- I cherish my spirit.
- I am connected to the divine.
- The wisdom of the universe flows in me.
- I trust and follow my intuition.
- I love and accept myself.
- I am at peace.
- My life is graceful.

- I live my life in the present.
- I seek experiences that nurture my spirit.
- I am thankful for everything good in my life.

Reconnect With Yourself

Reconnecting with yourself is a great way to bring your crown chakra back into alignment. To do this, focus on what you want out of life, listen to your inner voice, and allow your intuition to guide you through life. In order for your inner voice to express itself, however, you need to make sure that there is no room for negativity in your life.

CHAPTER NINE: HOW THE CHAKRAS INTERACT

In the preceding chapters, we have looked at each of the seven chakras and the techniques to heal the chakras in isolation. However, it is good to note that the chakras do not work in isolation; collectively, they are the chakra system for a reason. This is because they are all supposed to work together and in harmony with each other to ensure the optimal functioning of the whole *you*. Whenever one chakra is out of alignment, it will influence all the other chakras. This interdependence and intimate connection between the chakras means that we can't think about the chakras each on their own. Whenever you think of their effect on your physical, emotional, and mental wellbeing, think of them as an interconnected system.

Your body consists of energy and is designed to keep energy flowing at all times. This means that the body is constantly trying to find ways for energy to move in and out. If one chakra becomes blocked, your body still needs a way for that energy to flow, so it will excessively **open another chakra to compensate for the blocked chakra**. This response of compensating for one misalignment creates an even *greater* misalignment; instead of one, you now have two chakras out of alignment. Another chakra might also need to compensate for the misalignment of these two chakras, causing even further misalignment. What this means is that, if you want your chakras to remain healthy and well-balanced, focus on making sure that you have them all aligned, rather than focusing on one or two and forgetting about the rest.

It's also good to note that despite the chakras being arranged in a vertical line, and with each chakra influencing a different sphere of your life, there is no one chakra that is more important than the others. For instance, you cannot say that you don't mind having less energy in the throat chakra considering you have more energy in the root chakra because the latter is the foundation of the other chakras. Similarly, you don't want to have more energy in the third eye chakra and less energy in the heart chakra. This does *not* work. Instead, you want all the chakras to be equally open and aligned, allowing the optimal flow of energy into and out of each one of them.

Since we started discussing the chakras from the root chakra, you might also want to assume that energy in the chakras flows only in one direction; however, the energy flows in *both* directions. On the one hand, we have energy flowing in from the Earth through the root chakra and upwards to the other chakras. This provides us with stability and allows us to tap into the power of our ancestors and heritage. We also have the spiritual energy from the universe, which flows into us through the crown chakra and downwards through the other chakras. The root chakra then helps us ground this spiritual energy to the Earth, just like a lightning arrestor grounds electricity from the clouds to the Earth.

The channel that allows the back and forth flow of energy between the root and the crown chakras is known as **Sushumna**, which translates to "the central power current" or "the vertical power current." Once we have gained complete mastery of the Sushumna and can generate energy at the highest level, it becomes possible for us to summon **Kundalini** energy, also known as the "sleeping dragon" or "serpent." Kundalini is a rush of energy that surges from the first chakra to the seventh chakra with lots of power and allows us to achieve enlightenment.

While I said that no chakra is more important than the other, it is good to note that some chakras are more closely linked compared to others owing to the emotions and characteristics they control, meaning a blockage in one will highly affect the other. These blockages will then move on to affect *other* chakras that aren't so close-linked to the one with the blockage. For instance, we can take the root and crown chakras, which both link closely to each other; it is the responsibility of the root chakra to connect you to reality, while the crown chakra allows you to access experiences in dimensions that do not exist in the real world. You cannot experience higher realms of consciousness without a strong connection to reality. This will cause your connection to reality being severed, something that can lead to mental disturbances.

The close link between the crown and the root chakra is also consistent with the concept of *as above so below*. According to this concept, there is a direct relationship between what goes on between the upper and the lower chakras. Under this concept, the highest chakra links closely to the lowest chakra, and so on. Here, the crown chakra links closely to what happens in the root chakra, what happens in the third eye chakra connects to what happens in the sacral chakra, and what happens in the throat chakra can influence what happens in the solar plexus chakra. Therefore, blockage in the third eye chakra will affect the sacral chakra, then affect the solar plexus chakra, and so on.

Under the concept of *as above so below*, the heart chakra does not pair with another chakra because it acts as a point of connection and integration between the lower chakras, which concern with materialism and Earthly matters, and the upper chakras, which focus more on spirituality and higher aspirations.

Aside from the connection between what goes on between the upper and the lower chakras, there is also a close connection in how the elements of associated chakra complement each other. For instance, the element for the solar plexus chakra is fire, while the element for the heart chakra is air. In order for fire to burn fiercely, it needs air. Similarly, in order for one to be passionate (from the solar plexus chakra), they need love (from the heart chakra), and to be passionate, one needs love. It all shows how the two chakras are interdependent on each other.

CHAPTER TEN: THE HERO'S JOURNEY AND THE CHAKRA SYSTEM

Since the moment of our birth, we all have the potential to become heroes in our own life story. We all have an adventure, purpose, or journey that we are meant to take to grow spiritually and gain self-knowledge. This destined adventure shows us that there is more to life than just living from day to day and dying at the end. However, to be heroes in our lives, we have to decide whether we will take up our quest.

Before you head on your quest, you will need a map and an inner guide to ensure that you are heading in the right direction. The chakra system acts as your map and inner guide, setting you on the right path towards finding and fulfilling your life's purpose and discovering your true authentic self.

Essentially, we can describe the journey to find your true purpose in life and achieve knowledge and spiritual enlightenment as the journey from the *root chakra* to the *crown chakra*. Just like the journey to spiritual enlightenment takes the better part of a lifetime, so does the journey from the root chakra to the crown chakra.

Therefore, as you embark on a journey to balance your seven chakras, be fully cognizant of the fact that achieving fully activated and healthy chakras is something that will take the better part of your lifetime. Don't practice the techniques discussed within this book, hoping that you will align all the chakras in your body within a single month. Doing so will only set yourself up for failure because you will give up after seeing no changes within the short-term.

The key to activating and balancing all your seven chakras lies in being patient and positive-minded. Focus on one chakra, starting with the root chakra, and practice the techniques associated with that chakra until you fully activate and align it. Once the root chakra is well-aligned, move on to the sacral chakra and work on it until it also well-aligned and activated, after which you can move to the solar plexus chakra. Only by working progressively on each chakra, with patience and enthusiasm, will you be able to activate and balance all seven chakras.

Besides symbolizing your journey towards achieving knowledge and spiritual enlightenment, the seven chakras also represent the **life stages** that every person goes through while growing up. According to yogic philosophy, we go through **seven cycles** through our lifetime, each of which corresponds to one of the **seven chakras**. These seven cycles last seven years each; for instance, during your first seven years, the root chakra has the greatest influence in your life, after which the sacral chakra becomes more influential for the next seven years, and so on.

While going through each **seven-year cycle**, you also go through another **seven chakra ladder**, starting from the root chakra to the crown chakra. After completing the seven chakra ladder, you move on to the next seven-year cycle. In the 7 chakra ladder, the chakras are associated with the following themes:

- Root Chakra: Fear
- Sacral Chakra: Feelings
- Solar Plexus Chakra: Proactivity
- Heart Chakra: Harmony
- Throat Chakra: Philosophy
- Third Eye Chakra: Wisdom
- Crown Chakra: Spirituality

The following sections outline how the seven cycles affect our lives.

Age 0 – 7: The Root Chakra Cycle

The **root chakra** influences the first seven years of life. This is the period when one develops a sense of belonging and grounding. In the first year of life, you are also in the **first step** of the seven chakra ladder, associated with **fear**, and therefore your only goal at this stage is to **survive**.

At two years, while the root chakra is still the major source of influence, you are also in the second step of the chakra ladder—the sacral chakra—and therefore you develop feelings towards those who give you a sense of belonging; your parents or guardians. You also start developing likes, dislikes, and preferences.

At three years, you are still in the root chakra cycle, but in the third step of the chakra ladder—the solar plexus chakra. Here, you observe the world and gain a sense of self and who you are in relation to those around you.

At four years, still in the root chakra cycle, but now the heart chakra affects you. At this stage, you become more sociable and find joy in communicating with others.

At five years, you get into the throat chakra year, associated with philosophy. At this stage, you try to understand the world better and articulate yourself better. It is at this point that many children start their education.

At six years, while still in the root chakra cycle, the third eye chakra affects you, which associates with wisdom. At this stage, you understand yourself better and attempt to transfer your knowledge to others.

At seven years, you enter the last year of the root chakra cycle. This year is also influenced by the crown chakra associated with spirituality. This is the stage at which a child develops a curiosity about the mysterious nature of the world.

Age 8 – 14: The Sacral Chakra Cycle

In the midst of the **sacral chakra** cycle, the individual learns more about their emotions and how to express them, while also experiencing their **sexual energy** for the very first time. This is the stage at which girls get their first menstruation, and is also the time when most children develop their first "crushes."

At eight years, both the sacral and root chakras influence the child. They do not fully understand the desires they are experiencing and therefore have some feelings of fear towards these desires.

At nine years, the sacral chakra will influence the child in both dimensions. They experience feelings of love no longer directed at their parents. This is the age when most have their first crush.

At ten years, the child is in the solar plexus year of their sacral chakra cycle. Since this stage is associated with proactivity, they try to establish their first romantic relationship.

At 11 years, the child moves to the heart chakra stage of the sacral chakra cycle. This stage is associated with harmony. Driven by their feelings, the child will start exploring different friendships.

At 12 years, the child is under the influence of the sacral chakra and the throat chakra, associated with philosophy. This is the point where they understand the philosophy of love and friendship.

At 13 years, they get into their third eye chakra year of the sacral chakra cycle, and they gain an understanding of morality, honesty, and loyalty.

At 14 years, which is the final year of the sacral chakra cycle, the child tries to find greater meaning in their relationships with other people.

Age 15 – 21: Solar Plexus Chakra

In this stage, the **solar plexus chakra** influences the person, associated with **self-understanding** and **self-identity**. This is where teens understand their personalities better and what they want out of life.

At 15 years, most teenagers are getting into a period of proactivity in life. They are in the root chakra year of this cycle, so they also experience some fears about what the future holds.

At 16 years, both the solar plexus chakra (proactivity) and the sacral chakra (feelings) influence you. This is the point where you become more active in love and romantic relationships.

At 17 years, the solar plexus chakra influences you in both dimensions, and you might fall selfishly in love, in which the selfish desire to enjoy another person drives most of your actions.

At 18 years, you get into the heart chakra year of this cycle, when you crave a greater understanding of life, happiness, people, and relationships.

At 19 years, the solar plexus and throat chakras influence you, and you develop your own philosophies about things like family, love, and so on.

At 20 years, you get into the third eye year of the sacral chakra cycle. This is the point where you can test the philosophies you developed in real life, which results in wisdom.

At 21 years, you get into the crown chakra year, in which you are more concerned with spirituality. You will search for a partner with whom you can have a spiritual connection.

Age 22 – 28: The Heart Chakra Cycle

This is the stage where we really learn how to give and receive **love**. During this stage, most of us will meet our life partners and get married. Most people also think about the impact they will make in the world.

At 22 years, the first year of the heart chakra cycle is filled with fear (root chakra year). This could be the fear of not finding a life partner or the fear of committing to someone for life.

At 23 years, the heart and sacral chakras influence life, and the young adult understands and respects the feelings of other people around them.

At 24 years, the young adult gets into the proactivity year of the heart chakra phase, and they start paying greater focus to all aspects of their life. They also become more attuned to the needs of their family members.

At 25 years, the heart chakra is at play in both dimensions, and the young adult starts experiencing harmony and stability in all spheres of life. At this stage, it might feel like life has stagnated, leading to boredom.

At 27 years, the year of wisdom, the person develops their philosophies about family life and parenting.

At 28 years, the year of spirituality, you become more concerned with impacting the world and ensuring you have set up your children's lives for the future (the second if applicable).

Age 29 – 35: Throat Chakra Cycle

Philosophy influences this stage. This is the stage where most of us find our voices and learn how to express ourselves openly and freely. This is also the time when most people discover their **life's purpose**.

At 29 years, a person experiences some fear because of an uncertainty of the future.

At 30 years, the year of feelings, the person learns that they can achieve happiness by ensuring their feelings are in harmony.

At 31 years, philosophy and proactivity come into play as influences. This is where you develop your reason and start justifying your actions in life.

At 32 years, the year of harmony, you find ways of incorporating your life's purpose into your work.

At 33 years, the throat chakra influences both dimensions of your life. This is where you discover the philosopher in you.

At 34 years, the year of wisdom, you change your work and personal life to achieve happiness.

At 35 years, the final year of the throat chakra cycle, you try to bring spiritual development in all spheres of your life.

Age 36 – 42: Third Eye Chakra Cycle

This is the point where most people experience **epiphanies** and try to find a sense of **balance** in their lives. Many people become dogmatic at this point because of an unbalanced third eye chakra.

At 36 years, influenced by both the third eye chakra and the root chakra, fear that they might lose their balance in life fills the individual's mind and body.

At 37 years, which is the age of wisdom and feelings, the person tries to control their senses and perceptions.

At 38 years, the age of wisdom and proactivity, the person seeks other people who have achieved wisdom and spiritual enlightenment.

At 39 years, the age of wisdom and harmony, the individual comes into harmony with their wisdom.

At 40 years, wisdom and philosophy appear as influences. The individual spends their time in this stage sharing their wisdom with others.

At 41 years, wisdom is at play in both dimensions. This is the point where one attains true wisdom.

At 42 years, one ties the wisdom they have gained to God and spirituality.

Age 42 – 49: The Crown Chakra Cycle

This is the last cycle where life becomes concerned with **spirituality** and the need to understand the universe. Those with a blocked crown chakra fear death. This is also the point where most people experience the **mid-life crisis**.

At 43 years, the individual has many fears about God and spirituality.

At 44 years, the person incorporates their feelings into spirituality and finds spiritual pleasure.

At 45 years, the person becomes actively seeking a greater understanding of spirituality.

At 46 years, the individual achieves harmony in their spirituality.

At 47 years, the person understands the philosophy of having a spiritual life.

At 48 years, the age of spirituality and wisdom, the individual shares their spiritual wisdom with others.

At 49 years, when spirituality influences both dimensions, the person attains full spiritual enlightenment.

The above cycles represent the progression we go through in life as we progress on our hero's journey towards self-knowledge and spiritual enlightenment. This will not happen within the same timeframes for every person; some might take longer to move from one stage to another compared to others. This is just a general explanation of how these cycles work.

FINAL WORDS

This was quite a ride, and I'm glad you could stick with it to the end. By now, I hope you have learned so much about the chakra system and are now ready to apply this information to make a deeper connection with your mind, body, and soul, and improve your life.

The following is a recap of everything else you have learned in this book.

The concept of chakras originated in ancient **India** between 1500 and 500 BC and was first mentioned in the **Vedas** and the **Upanishads**.

The root chakra, also known as the **Mooladhara**, is at the base of the spine and is responsible and makes us feel **grounded** and ensuring our **survival**. A well-aligned root chakra increases your passion and vitality, makes you feel at ease and fearless, increases your sexual drive, and leads to financial abundance. An unbalanced Mooladhara leads to insecurity, obsession with money, greed, mistrust, low self-confidence, fear, low sexual drive, and a slew of physical symptoms. Fortunately, you can heal the root chakra through meditation, yoga, grounding, connecting with the Earth, using affirmations, using chakra stones, engaging in physical activity, and so on.

The sacral chakra, also referred to as **Svadhisthana**, is about two fingers above your coccyx and is associated with your **emotional responses**, your **creativity**, and your **sensuality**. An open sacral chakra results in a healthy relationship with your emotions, healthy relationships with others, and increased creativity. When blocked, your sacral chakra leads to negative and destructive emotions, addictions, excessive fantasizing, lack of fulfillment, codependence, low or excessive libido, and many physical problems. You can heal the sacral chakra through meditation, hip-opening yoga poses, affirmations, changing your diet, using chakra stones, connecting with water, dancing, abandoning toxic relationships, channeling your creativity, engaging in sensual sex, and so on.

The solar plexus chakra, also referred to as **Manipura**, is in the solar plexus and forms the core of a person's **identity**, **personality**, and **ego**. A well-aligned Manipura is associated with confidence, a clear sense of self, ability to set goals, persistence and determination, and assertiveness. An unbalanced Manipura leads to a victim mentality, overcompensation, people-pleasing actions, sensitivity to criticism, lack of ambition, and various physical symptoms. You can heal the Manipura through meditation, going after new experiences, affirmations, yoga, spending time outside, avoiding negative people, using chakra stones, and changing your diet.

The heart chakra, also referred to as **Anahata**, is near your heart and is responsible for your ability to give and receive **love** and form **relationships**. When your heart chakra is well-aligned, you bond well with other people, are full of love, altruistic, and full of respect for yourself and others. When your heart chakra is not aligned, you have trouble expressing your emotions, hold on to grudges, cannot move on from relationships, have trust issues, push people away, and experience a slew of physical symptoms. You can heal your heart chakra through meditation, affirmations, heart-opening yoga poses, adding green to your life, using chakra stones, changing your diet, showing gratitude and kindness, and being empathetic.

The throat chakra, also referred to as **Vishuddha**, is in the throat and is responsible for **communication** and the **ability to express** yourself. When your throat chakra is well-aligned, you are confident, have no trouble expressing yourself, and are a good listener. When this chakra is out of alignment, you struggle to express yourself, lose confidence, become unable to speak up for yourself, become shy, and experience some physical symptoms. You can heal the throat chakra through meditation, affirmations, yoga, chakra stones, adding blue into your life, getting a neck massage, and expressing your feelings.

The third eye chakra, also referred to as **Ajna**, is between your eyes and is the center of our **foresight** and **intuition**. When your third eye chakra is well-aligned, you can think logically and trust your instincts. You also achieve a clarity of purpose. When your third eye chakra is out-of-balance, you feel lost in life, have a negative imagination, experience endless frustration, and might experience several physical symptoms. You can heal your third eye chakra through meditation, yoga, affirmations, chakra stones, exploring different perspectives, observing your thoughts, and changing your limiting beliefs.

FINAL WORDS

The crown chakra, also referred to as **Sahasrara**, is at the top center of the head and grants you access to higher states of **consciousness** and **spiritual wisdom**. When your crown chakra is balanced, you unlock profound levels of clarity and inner peace, feel connected to the universe and to other people, and see the beauty in everything around you. When this chakra is unbalanced, you feel you have no direction, become spiritually disconnected, become lonely, find it hard to trust others and your intuition, experience boredom and frustration, and may even suffer from mental illnesses. You can heal your crown chakra through meditation, yoga, chakra stones, affirmations, and reconnecting with yourself.

The information from this book will arm you with all the knowledge you need to bring balance and harmony into your chakras and start reaping the benefits of the chakra system. However, keep in mind that for this to be effective, focus on achieving balance in *all* the seven chakras, not just a few. You should be patient, since achieving a balance of all your chakras will take some time. Otherwise, with practice and hard work, you will tap into the massive power of the chakra system.

All you need to do now is to put all of this into practice, and you will be on your way to aligning your mind, body, and soul and living a happy, meaningful life full of fulfillment and spiritual alignment.

REFERENCES

Basu, S. C. (Editor). (1880s). *Sabhâpati Swâmy* [Painting]. Published in *Lahore: Civil and Military Gazette Press*, 1880.

Bulaki. (Artist). (1823). *Chakras of the Subtle Body* [Painting]. Retrieved from http://www.britishmuseum.org/whats_on/past_exhibitions/2009/indian_summer/garden_and_cosmos.aspx

Chakra (2019). In *Wikipedia*. Retrieved from https://en.wikipedia.org/wiki/Chakra

Chek, P. (2019). *The chakra series — Part 5* [Video file]. Retrieved from https://www.youtube.com/watch?v=6VpPnU84kqE

Chek, P. (2019). *The chakra system part 2* [Video file]. Retrieved from https://www.youtube.com/watch?v=yvU11Q5eE3E

Chek, P. (2019). *The chakra system part 3* [Video file]. Retrieved from https://www.youtube.com/watch?v=3lkusUT4B4M

REFERENCES

Chek, P. (2019). *The chakra system part 4* [Video file]. Retrieved from https://www.youtube.com/watch?v=aLJ3J4NNHbE

Chek, P. (2019). *The chakra system 6* [Video file]. Retrieved from https://www.youtube.com/watch?v=tdNNxd34flU

Chek, P. (2019). *The chakra system — Part 7* [Video file]. Retrieved from https://www.youtube.com/watch?v=Tn76sP65xhs

Chek, P. (2019). *The chakra system: Transforming pain and bondage to freedom — Part 1* [Video file]. Retrieved from https://www.youtube.com/watch?v=AQtCtZxk-RM

Chou, W. (2019). 32 famous celebrities and successful people who meditate: The ultimate list. *Will's Personal-Devlopment Show*. Retrieved from https://willyoulaugh.com/celebrities-who-meditate/

Fernros, L., Furhoff, A.-K., & Wändell, P. E. (2018). Improving quality of life using compound mind-body therapies: Evaluation of a course intervention with body movement and breath therapy, guided imagery, chakra experiencing and mindfulness meditation. *Quality of Life Research, 17*(3), 367-376. doi:10.1007/s11136-008-9321-x

Gallegos, E. S. (1983). Animal imagery, the chakra system and psychotherapy. *Journal of Transpersonal Psychology, 15*(2), 125-136.

Gavin Flood. (2019). In *Wikipedia*. Retrieved from https://en.wikipedia.org/wiki/Gavin_Flood

Georg Feuerstein. (2019). In *Wikipedia*. Retrieved from https://en.wikipedia.org/wiki/Georg_Feuerstein

REFERENCES

Grimes, J. A. (1996). *A concise dictionary of indian philosophy*. Albany, NY: SUNY Press.

Helton, D. (2017). *Chakra meditation: Activating, clearing, & grounding the 1st chakra* [Video file]. Retrieved from https://www.youtube.com/watch?v=r9fKGbAFIf4

Judith, A. (2012). *Wheels of life: A user's guide to the chakra system*. Woodbury, MN: Llewellyn Worldwide.

Judith, A., & Anodea, J. (2004). *Eastern body, western mind: Psychology and the chakra system as a path to the self*. Berkeley, CA: Celestial Arts.

Kazlev, A. M. (2004). *The Chakras*. Retrieved from http://www.kheper.net/topics/chakras/index.html

Kazlev, A. M. (2004). The Shakta Theory of chakras. *Kheper*. Retrieved from http://www.kheper.net/topics/chakras/chakras-Shakta.htm

Maxwell, R. W. (2009). The physiological foundation of yoga chakra expression. *Zygon®, 44*(4), 807-824.

Meditative Mind. (2016). *Chakra healing guided meditation: Healing camp #1* [Video file]. Retrieved from https://www.youtube.com/watch?v=JTqktSAmG30

Meditative Mind. (2016). *Crown chakra healing guided meditation: Healing camp 2016: Day #7* [Video file] Retrieved from https://www.youtube.com/watch?v=7ZpUUXNQW1E

Meditative Mind. (2016). *Heart chakra healing guided meditation: Healing camp #4* [Video file]. Retrieved from https://www.youtube.com/watch?v=tDWoIAITBiY

Meditative Mind. (2016). *Sacral chakra healing guided meditation: Healing camp #2* [Video file]. Retrieved from https://www.youtube.com/watch?v=VRGs0GiR-QY

Meditative Mind. (2016). *Solar plexus chakra healing guided meditation: Healing camp #3* [Video file]. Retrieved from https://www.youtube.com/watch?v=Pz47Fv_TQDU

Meditative Mind. (2016). *Third eye chakra healing guided meditation: Healing camp 2016: Day #6* [Video file]. Retrieved from https://www.youtube.com/watch?v=IpbXlN2duKk

Meditative Mind. (2016). *Throat chakra healing guided meditation: Healing camp 2016: Day #5* [Video file]. Retrieved from https://www.youtube.com/watch?v=QwzSOF9GEHo

Meditative Mind. (2016). *Unblock all 7 chakras: Guided meditation: Healing camp 2016: Day 16* [Video file]. Retrieved from https://www.youtube.com/watch?v=4C0laqf93fg

Mookerjee, A. (1600s). *The subtle body and the cosmic man* [Painting]. Retrieved from http://www.artgallery.nsw.gov.au/sub/goddess/education.html

Nepalese Painting, 18th century. (1800). [Painting]. Retrieved from http://www.kheper.net/topics/chakras/chakras-Shakta.htm

Selby, J., & Selig, Z. (2009). *Kundalini awakening: A gentle guide to chakra activation and spiritual growth*. New York City, NY: Bantam Books.

Sharamon, S., & Baginski, B. (2018). *Chakra handbook*. Twin Lakes, WI: Lotus Press.

Simpson, L. (1999). *The book of chakra healing*. New York City, NY: Sterling Publishing Company, Inc.

Smart, R. [Infinite Waters (Diving Deep)]. (2016). *How to open and balance the 7 chakras (the secret)* [Video file]. Retrieved from https://www.youtube.com/watch?v=As6aauMZ93M

REFERENCES

Smart, R. [Infinite Waters (Diving Deep)]. (2015) *How to open your 7 chakras: The science of the chakras* [Video file]. Retrieved from https://www.youtube.com/watch?v=dfIuSSA_27w

Smart, R. [Infinite Waters (Diving Deep)]. (2017). *How to open your 7 chakras: The science of the chakras & chakra healing* [Video file]. Retrieved from https://www.youtube.com/watch?v=qt7APLdT0cM

Smart, R. [Infinite Waters (Diving Deep)]. (2019). *How to unblock all 7 chakras and trust the universe [warning — **life changing**]* [Video file]. Retrieved from https://www.youtube.com/watch?v=QN99kqVFQCk

Swan, T. (2013). *How to activate and open your third eye — Teal Swan* [Video file]. Retrieved from https://www.youtube.com/watch?v=KDnBw7EXa3w&list=PLAtqcnCw8YZxj0313Vp5167S_3ZOw8Hc1&index=6

Swan, T. (2013). *How to ground yourself (All about grounding) — Teal Swan* [Video file]. Retrieved from https://www.youtube.com/watch?v=glHYP8j3fiY&list=PLAtqcnCw8YZxj0313Vp5167S_3ZOw8Hc1&index=2

Swan, T. (2015). *How to open your crown chakra* [Video file]. Retrieved from https://www.youtube.com/watch?v=2TxJDLDO3rI&list=PLAtqcnCw8YZxj0313Vp5167S_3ZOw8Hc1&index=7

Swan, T. (2016). *How to open your heart chakra — Teal Swan -* [Video file]. Retrieved from https://www.youtube.com/watch?v=L4bKficC1ag&list=PLAtqcnCw8YZxj0313Vp5167S_3ZOw8Hc1&index=4

REFERENCES

Swan, T. (2018). *How to open your sacral chakra — Teal Swan* [Video file]. Retrieved from https://www.youtube.com/watch?v=Nlys9wo-bvs&list=

PLAtqcnCw8YZxj0313Vp5167S_3ZOw8Hc1&index=1

Swan, T. (2018). *How to open your solar plexus chakra — Teal Swan* - [Video file]. Retrieved from https://www.youtube.com/watch?v=dwaR-7ygoWE&list=

PLAtqcnCw8YZxj0313Vp5167S_3ZOw8Hc1&index=3

Swan, T. (2017). *How to open your throat chakra — Teal Swan* - [Video file]. Retrieved from https://www.youtube.com/watch?v=uAFO8xsA7Hk&list=PLAtqcnCw8YZxj0313Vp5167S_3ZOw8Hc1&index=5

The Editors of Encyclopaedia Britannica. (2018). Chakra. Retrieved from https://www.britannica.com/topic/chakra

The Editors of Encyclopaedia Britannica. (2014). Chakravartin. In *Encyclopaedia Britannica*. Retrieved from https://www.britannica.com/topic/chakravartin

Valuetainment. (2019). *Why Kobe is loyal to Phil Jackson* [Video file]. Retrieved from https://www.youtube.com/watch?v=IIj8n3-u3ag

Yoga International. (n.d.). What are the 7 chakras?: Learn more about the 7 main chakras. *Yoga International*. Retrieved from https://yogainternational.com/article/view/what-are-the-7-chakras#

ACKNOWLEDGMENTS

Image Credit: Shutterstock.com

Made in the USA
Middletown, DE
13 December 2019